Ask.

Ask.

The counterintuitive online formula to discover *exactly* what your customers want to buy… create a mass of raving fans… and take *any* business to the next level

RYAN LEVESQUE

DUNHAM
books

Publishing support, design, and composition by Coachzing: Marketing and publishing solutions for busy professionals. www.coachzing.com.

Library of Congress Control Number: 2015931330

Trade Paperback ISBN: 978-1-939447-72-2

E-book ISBN: 978-1-939447-73-9

Printed in the United States of America

TABLE OF CONTENTS

DEDICATION

Dedicated to my wife, Tylene, who has supported me each step of the way, and without whom none of this would have been possible. And to my two incredible sons, Henry and Bradley, who are my inspiration every single day. I love you all more than words will ever express.

FOREWORD

"That's it!" we both echoed in triumphant agreement after a 12-hour marathon hike on July 18th, 2011. After 28 years pursuing the ultimate marketing formula, it all seemed so simple, so elegant, so perfect.

But it took someone like my student and good friend, Ryan Levesque, to make it so... and a very painful 18-mile trek in the White Mountains of New Hampshire with no email, cell phone, or other distractions to articulate the concept in its purest form.

Of course, we both knew the devil was in the details, but how could the formula *itself* be so simple? Well... it is.

Let's start at the beginning...

I believe it was the day after Christmas, 2008, when I signed for the FedEx envelope at my door. "That's weird," I thought. "Who the heck sends a FedEx on Christmas Day?" But then it occurred to me: "Pretty darn slick... because how can I possibly NOT open and read it now that the sender has piqued my curiosity?"

Inside was a passionately written letter with a $100 bill neatly stapled to the top. There was also a $500 cashier's check made out to my company.

It seems that Ryan was intent on paying for my coaching services, and the fact that I had a big "Closed" sign on the website, which informed people of the long waiting list, wasn't going to stop him. Of course, I politely returned his money and let him know where he could sign up for the list. (*He was the first one to sign up a few months later, when I had an opening.*)

In retrospect, the FedEx experience was a foreshadowing of things to come with Ryan. I've long since learned trying to stop him from accomplishing anything is entirely fruitless.

Whether it's getting the attention *of someone whose attention does not want getting*, climbing the tallest mountain, or figuring out how to overcome the most difficult of marketing challenges, Ryan is probably the most determined person I've ever met...

Ryan will do *exactly* what everyone else says can't be done—or isn't willing to do—and then he'll figure out how to systematize it so it becomes a lot easier to implement than everyone else thinks!

Ryan succeeds where others fail because of his keen intellect, ravenous appetite for the truth, penchant for detail, persistence, and, perhaps above all else, his willingness to "play the long game" until he patches every last hole in his master formula.

But before I tell you too much about why Ryan is the only person who could have possibly written this book, I should let you know WHY you'll want to read it from cover to cover in the first place...

In other words, what's in it for YOU, dear reader?

Exactly this: The world's most powerful marketing formula, which YOU can use to dramatically improve the bottom-line profits in your business. That's what! (*In my not-so-humble-and-painfully-considered opinion.*)

Now, please know I don't make this statement lightly. In fact, it's actually a statement against my own best interest:

- I've been an aggressive student of marketing for more than 28 years. My wife and I have sold more than $30,000,000 in marketing consulting to Fortune 100 companies like Lipton, American Express, Colgate-Palmolive, Whirlpool, Panasonic, AT&T, Kodak, Hallmark, and more. (In fact, we've worked with literally dozens of Fortune 500 companies...)
- Along the way our work, research, and theories have been covered in major media like the *New York Times*, the *Los Angeles Times*, the *Chicago Sun Times*, the *New York Daily News*, *Crain's New York Business*, the *Milwaukee Business Journal*, the *Indiana Star Ledger*, *American Demographics*, CBS & ABC Radio, Bloomberg Radio, WGN and UPN TV, and many, many more.
- I co-founded (and eventually sold) an Internet marketing agency that managed millions in online advertising, developed and distributed marketing education programs to an international audience of thousands, and has seen the dollars-in-to-dollars-out results of hundreds of business models.
- I'm also in regular contact with some of the top marketing and branding experts in the world.

I should have written this book myself... but I didn't, because—*as much as I'm embarrassed to admit it*—there were a few missing pieces to my formula which only Ryan could have figured out—critical missing pieces that made it difficult to implement on the much grander and more effective scale that Ryan has now proven, pieces I should have seen but didn't.

Ryan's formula is the "finished product"... the polished piece. And God bless him for doing it... Because I'd now put Ryan up against anyone in the world marketing in the same arena. Anyone—*including me*!

Now, I've been very successful implementing, teaching, and profiting from version 1.0 of the "*Ask Formula*" on my own. And I had quite a reputation... because I'd entered more than a dozen markets profitably and consecutively right out of the gate.

Ryan studied this formula more intensely than any of my other students. To say he was obsessed would be an understatement. He repeatedly flew out to my house to talk to me about it. He used it to develop his own very profitable business (*in an arena which had nothing to do with teaching others to make money, by the way...*).

And then he asked—*which is my polite way of saying "begged"*—to handle the overflow of consulting clients on my waiting list so he could get even more experience. I had only glowing reviews from the clients I sent him, at which point I asked if Ryan would do a marketing podcast series with me... another resounding success.

Slowly, as I got to know him better and better, I began to realize this "kid" was doing something with the formula I wasn't...

- Where I would be looking to conserve resources and find shortcuts because my implementation of the formula was rather laborious, he was instead asking how we could better systematize the process so we could shift the work to lower-cost labor.
- Ryan made a much more intensive study of copywriting than I did. As a result, he told better and more relevant stories. I'm admittedly still a bit of a "propeller-head professor." If I don't watch myself carefully, I'm prone to drone on about extremely valuable facts, which, although very useful for the prospect willing to study them, couldn't sell their way out of a paper bag. So, as much as I hate to admit it,

Ryan's sales copy and email follow-up messages were more powerful and engaging than my own. (*So much so that I actually consider myself a student of his in these regards now.*)

- Having observed the power of the "*Ask Formula*," Ryan took it to the Nth degree. (*That's Ryan for you!*)

Whereas I introduced the concept of the "*Ask Formula*," Ryan systematized it and refined it to a degree more than I had been previously willing to do, and in a more engaging and powerful way. Is it any wonder he quickly built a multimillion dollar agency with clients who are terrified of losing his service?

But you don't have to be a "Ryan Levesque" to benefit from this book. You only need an open mind and a willingness to implement SOME of this stuff on even the most basic level... Because 95% of your competitors probably never will!

—Glenn Livingston, Ph.D.
www.GlennLivingston.com

INTRODUCTION

HOW TO USE THIS BOOK

Dear Friend,

If you ask 1,000 entrepreneurs, business owners, or aspiring business owners to complete the sentence: *"I wish I had more _____."* Ninety-four percent will say one of two things.

The most common response is time.

The second most common response?

Well, that's something we'll get to in just a moment.

But first, when it comes to time, if your life is anything like mine, between work, family, and the ever-changing online landscape, there are times when it feels like there just aren't enough hours in the day.

As a dad, husband, and CEO (because my time is so limited) I'm increasingly picky about which business books I read. I suspect you might be particular about what you read as well. At the same time, I know that all it takes is just one pivotal idea for a book or resource to change my life forever.

I believe *Ask* is one of those resources truly worth the investment of your time.

And not only that...

When you apply what you're about to discover, the contents of this book can deliver the *second* most common thing entrepreneurs, business owners, and aspiring business owners say when asked to complete the "I wish I had more _____" sentence.

That thing?

Money.

The reason I say that is because, as you're about to discover, the *Ask Formula* is responsible for generating over $100 million in sales online—revolutionizing industries ranging from business funding to dog training.

And, in addition to the financial impact this formula is having in industry after industry, businesses *using* this formula are seeing their previously uninspired customers transform into *raving fans* and repeat buyers right before their eyes.

And most importantly, by the time you're finished with this book, the *Ask Formula* is something *you* will be able to use in *your* business.

But before we dive in, because I want you to get the most out of this book in the least amount of time, let me explain how *Ask* is organized.

This book is broken down into two main parts.

Part One of the book is the "behind the scenes" background story that tells you a little about who I am and how the *Ask Formula* came about. As I share with you some of the twists and turns of my (slightly unusual) journey to where the *Ask Formula* finally came together, my hope is that it provides you with three things...

First, context for what the *Ask Formula* is; second, a recognition of opportunities where the *Ask Formula* can be used; third, and perhaps most importantly, inspiration to hang in there when things are tough.

Every successful entrepreneur's story is filled with near-failure. My story is no different, and if you're like most people, I think you'll be surprised to hear how it took me almost dying for the *Ask Formula* to come into existence.

Part Two of the book is the "methodology" section, which shows you what the *Ask Formula* is and how to apply it in your business in step-by-step detail.

If you're the type of person who wants to skip the background and "cut to the chase," you can go straight to the methodology section and it's all laid out for you. Of course, after reading it, if you want to go back and find out how I came up with the formula, it may make even more sense. The choice is yours as to where to begin.

That said, wherever you start (with the story or methodology), this book is intentionally designed to be *interactive*.

What I mean by that is, by necessity, there is a blurring of offline and online worlds today. The days of a written book (or even ebook) being nothing but a "book" are long gone. More often than not, *concepts* are timeless, but with rapid changes in technology, the *application* of those concepts can change rapidly.

It is my goal to help you understand the timeless concepts and strategies in *Ask* and give you access to the most *up-to-date* application of those concepts at the same time.

For this reason, you will find "signposts" along the way in this book that will lead you to a secret bonus section of the *Ask Formula* website, *exclusively available* to you as a *reader*, which is designed to go hand in hand with this book.

This free secret bonus section includes critical updates, illustrations, and live examples I'll be referring to throughout the text to help show you how to apply the *Ask Formula* in your business and get results *fast*.

By the way, if you're curious to get a sneak peek of some of the goodies in this free secret bonus section right now, you can take a quick look now by visiting: http://www.AskFormula.com/bonuses. (Just please do me a favor, and don't share that link. It's for verified *readers* only.)

With that being said, at the same time I want to point out something that's super important. I want you to understand the *Ask Formula* is here in its *entirety*. I've held nothing back. It is all there for you to use and customize for your business. I've given you everything I can in the confines of one book to use the *Ask Formula* successfully. And at the end of the book, I explain why I decided to share my "secret family recipe" with the world like this, and hold nothing back.

So there you have it. The choice is yours. Start at the beginning or in the middle, whichever you prefer.

But whatever you decide, the important thing is to *start*. My team and I are committed to helping you understand the *Ask Formula* and give you everything you need and *more* to take your business to the next level.

So without further delay, let's get started!

—*Ryan Levesque*

Part I

ASK: THE STORY

CHAPTER ONE

You: Who, What, & Why...

Let me ask you a question.

If you were to Google "How many ads are we exposed to daily?" what do you think is the answer? Take a guess.

I was curious myself, so I searched and found that, according to CBS News, "We've gone from being exposed to about 500 ads a day back in the 1970's to as many as 5,000 a day today."[1]

That was in 2006.

Now that number may or may not be true, but I think we can all agree we're being bombarded with more advertising and marketing messages than ever before. And if we didn't tune them out, we wouldn't be able to function.

But, for some reason, in all this cacophony, marketers *still* seem to think if they can stand on their tippy toes, and scream loudly enough (metaphorically speaking), even strategically, they can get the attention of customers.

What I'm going to tell you is how, with a quiet, almost hushed voice, you can break through that cacophony and communicate with customers so they feel like you're talking *to* them and not *at* them.

And you can get them to (willingly) tell you what they want to buy, and more importantly, what they want to buy from *you*.

But, as you'll discover in a moment, to get an accurate answer to this question—it's *not* something you can ask directly. In other words, you *cannot* directly *ask* what people want. It

---

1. Cutting Through Advertising Clutter — CBS *Sunday Morning*

takes a somewhat counterintuitive approach that, when done right, can be *wickedly effective.*

I'm going to show you, in detail, my *Ask Formula*, the same formula my clients, customers, and I have used to quietly generate over 3 million leads and over 200,000 customers across 23 different major markets in just the past several years—generating well over $100 million dollars in revenue in the process.

My goal for you is that, after you discover this *Ask Formula* for yourself, you'll walk away with a specific, practical, step-by-step process you can immediately begin applying in your business, which will increase your income exponentially.

Now, if you're anything like me, whenever I read a new business book, the #1 question I'm asking myself is always: *"Is this something I'm going to be able to use in my business?"*

So to help you decide if this is something you can use in your business, here's the answer to the question: "Who is this for?"

- If you're thinking about starting a *new* business, launching a *new* product, or kicking off a *new* project with any sort of online presence, then this is for you.
- If you already *have* a business with an online presence and you've *struggled to convert cold traffic into customers*— whether that's traffic from Facebook, Google AdWords, YouTube videos, banner advertising, or any *other* cold traffic source—then this is for you.
- If you have an online business and you're tired of relying on affiliates or joint-venture promotions, or running internal launches, then, again, this is for you.
- If you simply want a proven, *evergreen* online sales model you can build once, "set it and forget it," and enjoy the type of passive income this formula is producing month after month, year after year, in market after market—then yes, this system is for you.
- And lastly, if you have or work with clients in any of those situations, then this is something you can use as well.

I'm going to show you what I consider to be the "Holy Grail" of online marketing: how to convert cold website traffic into *paying* customers in scale, consistently and reliably. And using a somewhat unconventional approach, I'll show you how to transform that traffic into predictable, recurring passive income for you and your business.

The secret to doing all this is contained within the pages of this book. I'm going to show you the exact path, the exact flow-chart, the exact strategy I've used to successfully enter those 23 different major markets—and making millions of dollars in the process, both for myself and the clients who work with my team and me. And, by the end of this book, you're going to be able to use this same proven strategy in your business, regardless of your product or service, and get results fast.

■ ■ ■

Some of the industries in which the *Ask Formula* has been applied with great success include sports instruction, satellite television, real estate, consumer financial services, business funding, educational programming, healthcare, and many more. But if I were in your shoes, I'd like to see some *proof* that what you're about to discover actually works.

So before we go any further, let me share with you how I—and marketers around the world—have been quietly using the *Ask Formula* to create massive growth for businesses large and small.

In my own company, I've used this formula to successfully enter and dominate obscure markets ranging from the Scrabble® tile jewelry market—a small "lifestyle" business that as you'll discover generated as much as $10,000 a month in income for my wife and me, to my award-winning RocketMemory™ course system in the memory-improvement market, which has helped over 26,000 people around the world in over 40 countries.

In fact, after struggling to generate *any* income in my first few attempts to build an online business, once I started dialing in and using the *Ask Formula* (the same one you're about to discover), I went from earning $370.88 to $24,275.99 per month within 18 months in what I describe as my first "real" online business. Today I own a publishing and marketing company that generates millions of dollars per year by applying the same formula in market after market. (Here's a screenshot from my 1ShoppingCart account of the first 18 months of that first Internet business.)

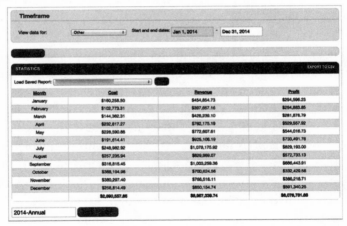

Month ▾	Orders Count ⇅	Gross Sales ⇅	Shipping ⇅	Taxes ⇅	Net Sales ⇅
November 2008	18	$370.88	$0.00	$0.00	$370.88
December 2008	40	$848.87	$0.00	$0.00	$848.87
January 2009	76	$1920.39	$0.00	$0.00	$1920.39
February 2009	70	$1888.39	$0.00	$0.00	$1888.39
March 2009	170	$4522.30	$340.00	$0.00	$4182.30
April 2009	274	$9515.93	$1250.00	$0.00	$8265.93
May 2009	382	$13850.79	$1750.00	$0.00	$12100.79
June 2009	392	$14085.87	$1790.00	$0.00	$12295.87
July 2009	317	$11155.53	$1450.00	$0.00	$9705.53
August 2009	426	$13480.96	$1995.00	$0.00	$11485.96
September 2009	371	$12391.24	$1715.00	$0.00	$10676.24
October 2009	413	$13273.44	$1990.00	$0.00	$11283.44
November 2009	420	$12618.73	$2015.00	$0.00	$10603.73
December 2009	416	$12788.55	$2020.00	$0.00	$10768.55
January 2010	637	$18271.44	$2940.00	$0.00	$15331.44
February 2010	835	$23893.88	$3645.00	$0.00	$20248.88
March 2010	842	$24275.99	$3485.00	$0.00	$20790.99
Grand Total	**6099**	**$189153.18**	**$26385.00**	**$0.00**	**$162768.18**

In fact, in certain markets we generate upwards of eight million dollars per year on individual product lines using the *Ask Formula*, as you can see here:

But more importantly, *other* business are having amazing success implementing this formula—and it far eclipses these numbers, to the tune of well over $100 million in revenue generated since the formula's inception. Later in this book, in the *Case Studies* section, you'll discover how one client—the tennis instruction website FuzzyYellowBalls.com—generated over $250,000 in revenue in under six months for what was a previously struggling product line, using the *Ask Formula*.

You'll also discover how another client—the alkaline health company LiveEnergized.com—generated over $750,000 in just *five days* selling a high-end water ionizer (which has since sold *millions* of dollars more). There are literally hundreds more businesses around the world using the formula you are about to discover to transform their business as we speak. And to give you a sense of the *immediate* impact this formula can have on your business, no matter how big or small your business is right now, here are just a handful of those hundreds of success stories from business owners around the world.

> *"Ryan's segmented email strategy generated an additional 75 sales in a single week, which represents an additional $15,000 in weekly revenue for our company..."*
> —Carla Corrigan, Sterling Satellite, Top 5 DISH® Network Affiliate, www.DishPromotions.com

> *"Previously, the best I could do was a 70% ROI on my sales funnel. By using the Ask Formula and Ryan's teachings I was able to more than double that number to a 150% ROI with about 12 weeks of work..."*
> —Brandon Schmid, President, Angelus Marketing, Barrie, ON Canada

> *"The* Ask Formula *and what Ryan Levesque teaches has helped increase our conversion and closing rate by about 15% just since implementing some of his teachings over the last 3 months..."*
> —David McGarry, CEO, Gym-Marketing Expert, Dallas, TX

> *"Using what Ryan teaches, we were able to create a sales funnel that's converting 250% better than our old sales video..."*
> —Jonathan Rivera, www.ThePodcastFactory.com

"Just applying a variation on the 'profit maximization' process Ryan teaches in the Ask Formula *added an extra $96,000 in profit to our business last year..."*
—Ronnie Nijmeh, CEO, www.PLR.me, Toronto, ON Canada

"The Survey Funnel Strategy *is producing a 40% year over year lift in revenue—and we still haven't fully optimized it..."*
—Darren Crawford, www.BeforeUnit.com, Melbourne Beach, Florida

"We used the Ask Formula *to launch a new business unit and grow from zero to $467,110 in our first six months online, and we're just getting started..."*
—Dan Meredith, CEO, Wellness Business Solutions, Bristol, UK

And this just scratches the surface. Now that you've gotten a sense for the type of results companies are getting using the *Ask Formula*, if you're like most people reading this, you're probably wondering...

Okay, so what exactly is the *Ask Formula*, and why does it work so well in market after market?

CHAPTER TWO

Strange Questions... and Stranger Answers

"It's really hard to design products by focus groups. A lot of times, people don't know what they want until you show it to them."
— STEVE JOBS

What is the *Ask Formula*?

Simply put, the *Ask Formula* is a system to ask intentionally-designed questions to help you figure out exactly what your customer wants—and the exact language to use to communicate with them. Then, with that information, it tells you how to personalize the messaging you use and products you introduce based on the answers to the questions you ask.

In other words, it's a way of discovering what your customer wants to buy by guiding them through a series of (somewhat counterintuitive) questions and customizing a solution for them so they are more likely to purchase from you. And it's a way to do it that is *completely automated* and does not require one-on-one conversations with every single customer.

THE PAYOFF IS *HUGE* IN THREE WAYS:

1. You get back priceless information to help you know what they want to buy and when they're ready to buy it. They'll become a happy customer who'll come back to buy, time and time again.
2. You find out why they *didn't* buy, providing opportunities to revise your campaign, fix your product or promotion, and reengage them so they'll eventually become that happy customer who returns to buy again and again.

3. Once optimized, it gives you the ability to *scale* your business significantly, limited only by the size of the market in which you operate.

Simple on the surface, but like most things in life—the devil is in the details.

I'll go into massive detail on the *Ask Formula* in the methodology section. But in plain English, the way to apply the *Ask Formula* online is by using a *unique combination of surveys in a very specific sequence, and acting on that data in a very specific way.*

For years—and to some extent, even to this day—for many people the word "survey" only conjured up images of irritating phone calls from telemarketers interrupting your dinner asking for your opinions, and that was it: no follow-up with results, no benefit to you, the survey-taker. They were designed by the marketer only to help the marketer.

But the new definition of "survey" is all about engagement and empowerment for both the marketer and customer. It's not just one-sided anymore. That's why this formula is so powerful and why, when the type of surveys you're about to discover are positioned properly, people are actually *very* motivated to take them. The secret? It's all about appealing to people's sense of self-discovery and curiosity—which is something we'll be talking about in Part Two of the book.

The *Ask Formula* is a series of surveys (or questions) designed to determine what a customer wants, along with customized sales language based on those answers to get that customer to buy. Think of it like a funnel. A funnel is a tube or pipe that is wide at the top and narrow at the bottom, used for guiding liquid or powder into a small opening.

A survey (or question) funnel operates the same way. You start by asking big wide questions at first, and then those questions narrow, and narrow more, as you ask your customers simple, more precise questions about their situation—until you have enough information to speak to their specific wants, needs, and desires.

After intensive testing and refining, I've come up with four basic survey types that comprise the *Ask Formula*, which we'll be covering in detail in the second half of the book. These are the core surveys that can be used for any online business with proven, and usually dramatic, results. They help you do four things: define your market, engage your market, refine your marketing, and redeem your marketing efforts.

Over the past eight years, I've devoted practically my entire professional life to asking people questions and creating streams of revenue from those answers. During that time, I've met a number of people who have said they've tried using surveys and haven't found them all that helpful. They just weren't making them money.

After probing a bit, I'm not surprised to find that they're asking the wrong questions the wrong way, and they're looking at the wrong data. Again, the devil is in the details.

I hate to say it, but when it comes to using surveys in ways that actually make money, most businesses just don't have a clue. Even the biggest businesses—the kind of companies you'd never expect to struggle with anything—seem to get surveys wrong.

It isn't their fault. When it comes to asking questions, whether they're a big corporation or a one-person boutique, business owners are prone to making the same costly mistake: *They try to just ask customers what they want.*

"What would you like to purchase on this site?"

"What kind of product do you want?"

"How can we help you?"

Sound familiar? Instinctively, *we ask people what they want.* We think if we just ask them, they'll tell us, and we can sit back and watch the dollars pour in.

If only it were that simple.

There's a famous quote that's been attributed to Henry Ford: "If I had asked people what they wanted, they would have said 'faster horses.'"

Now, the reason why this quotation rings true for so many people is because it *is true.*

People have been polling their potential customers for millennia, asking questions and trying to convert what they find into dollars. However, when questions are asked in this straightforward way... well, it usually ends in disappointment for the business owner.

Because (here's the big secret): *People don't know what they want.*

Really.

In fact, to illustrate this point, think about the last time you and a group of friends were hanging out and thinking about where to go out to eat. You're all sitting around and someone says, "Hey, anybody hungry? What do you all feel like doing for dinner?"

What's the most common response?

"I don't know. What do you want?"

Sometimes that conversation goes around in circles—endlessly.

Why? Because, at the end of the day, *people don't know what they want.*

However, if you're hanging out with that same group of friends and you can ask a different sort of question:

"Well, is there anything you *don't* feel like eating for dinner tonight?"

Interestingly, people are much better at answering that type of question.

Your friends might say, "I don't feel like pizza because I'm trying to eat gluten-free." or "I don't want to do sushi because I'm allergic to shellfish."

People are really good at telling you what it is they *don't* want.

Similarly, you can also ask each of your friends one by one, "What did you have for dinner last night?"

And people are also very good at answering *that* question as well.

The reason why is because people essentially are only good at answering *two* basic types of questions when they don't know what they want: What it is they *don't* want and what they've done in the *past.*

(This is true both online and offline, by the way.)

Vague, general asking is one of the biggest mistakes people make when trying to find out what people want. It's because people just don't know how to answer. Steve Jobs was right. People often *don't know* what will make their life better until they've seen it.

So then the question is: *What's the solution?*

Well, if we go back to the Henry Ford quotation, instead of asking people what they wanted, what if Ford had asked, "What is it that you *don't* like about horses?"

Chances are, he would have gotten back all sorts of useful information. People may have said things like, "I don't like the fact that my horse is slow or needs to be fed." Or "I don't like the fact that only one person can ride my horse at a time."

The point is, there are certainly things about horses that people didn't like, but they didn't know the solution was something outside of what they could imagine.

That's actually where the exciting part comes in. As entrepreneurs and marketers, we get to identify and provide that solution. But to create and sell something that people will actually buy, what you need is the raw material to extract from the market to determine what that solution is—even when your customers can't quite articulate it.

That's why, to get the type of results in market after market like you're about to see, it requires using surveys in a somewhat different, unexpected way.

Because the right way to use surveys is *counterintuitive*.

CHAPTER THREE

The Discovery

So how did I figure this all out? Well, quite frankly, it was a combination of intense study, hard work, and attending the entrepreneurial "school of hard knocks."

Strangely, I come from a corporate and academic background in neuroscience from Brown University. And I speak nearly fluent Chinese (that story's to come). And although I thought the corporate world would be for me, I had this deep longing to be an entrepreneur. Even as a kid, I created businesses, starting when I was 13.

In my mid-twenties, once I became a full-time entrepreneur (the "no turning back" kind), I set out to make my mark.

After failing in more than a few early attempts in the online marketing world, out of sheer frustration, I finally decided to ask people what they needed help with and why they didn't buy. Their answers surprised me, but they told me what I needed to hear.

One of the biggest things I discovered was that I had been taking a "one size fits all" approach to my marketing. Their responses told me I needed to speak to different segments of the market quite differently. Quite frankly, I asked out of necessity because I was desperate and didn't know how to succeed otherwise. But the result of the "desperation attempt" of my asking questions of the market became the foundation for a formula that I've personally used to successfully enter and dominate 23 different markets (and counting), that my customers and clients have used in *hundreds* of different markets, and that, when strategically and appropriately applied, can revolutionize practically any business—including yours.

It was after testing, testing, and more testing with my own businesses that I realized I had stumbled on a particular approach that anyone could replicate, if they were simply armed with the right information.

The *Ask Formula* I discovered was stunningly simple: The secret to spectacular sales was all about asking the *right* questions, in the *right* way, at the *right* time.

As I said, the discovery of how to ask the right questions, make money in the process, and have satisfied customers coming back for more is an area that's more nuanced and more misunderstood than it might initially seem. But after years of testing, sifting, and reviewing what works and what doesn't, I now have a proven formula that has worked in multiple businesses and made markets responsive that were previously considered dead.

The reason why I'm telling you all this is because I want to give you the confidence that the formula you're about to discover has been tested, battle-tested, and stress-tested in market after market. It has been used by companies both large and small, so you can have the confidence that this is something you can apply in your business.

Are you skeptical? Great. I consider myself a chief among skeptics.

So before I explain all the details and the methodology of the *Ask Formula*, I'd like to tell you a little bit about myself and the unlikely story of how the *Ask Formula* came together to create what's becoming a *movement* online—with a financial impact beyond my wildest imagination.

As I take you along my journey with its winding paths and pitfalls, even where I failed—and nearly lost it all—I think you'll come to understand better what the *Ask Formula* is, why it's so useful, and the dramatic impact it can make in your business.

CHAPTER FOUR

My Crisis

It was 2 a.m. on a cold morning in February of 2012 when I woke up to find myself slumped over a bag of potato chips, some chocolate-covered pretzels, a bowl of Cool Ranch Doritos—and a half-empty Red Bull.

I would've been slumped there all night if my wife hadn't walked in and woken me up.

She wasn't thrilled with me, to say the least. We were supposed to be taking turns standing sentinel over the crib of our brand new baby boy to make sure, like most new parents, that he didn't stop breathing.

You see, when we brought him home that night, born two weeks late, we were in a bit of "new parent shock." We couldn't believe this tiny, little person was now our responsibility.

We were totally in love with him and yet... we were clueless and pretty much terrified.

And so, that first night, my wife and I took turns staying up all night just watching him sleep. I offered to take first watch. So I set up camp in the baby's room with all the essentials (Doritos, Red Bull, etc.) plus a few action movies to keep myself awake when I wasn't checking on him.

I promised myself I wouldn't sleep.

But it wasn't long before I *did* fall asleep and only woke up when my wife walked in the nursery, finding me with my face practically planted in the Doritos. Great job, Dad.

The good news is that, somehow, my resilient son remained alive and breathing in his crib despite my constant nodding off. And quickly, he began to grow and thrive—but not so for me.

Over the next few months, it started feeling like something was "off." My inability to stay up that night was the first night of what eventually became a pattern. I knew what it felt like to be tired. I had pushed through many all-nighters in college and had burnt the candle on both ends many nights before.

But suddenly I started experiencing exhaustion like never before. I could barely give my son a bath at night, without having to sit down afterward. After I'd put him to bed, I'd sit on the couch motionless for hours just to catch my breath—even though I really wanted to get up and do something.

It wasn't that I was depressed. But normal everyday tasks just wiped me out. All I wanted to do was rest.

I chalked up the feeling of constant exhaustion to the fact that I was a new dad, running a fast-growing company, and not getting much sleep.

My wife noticed something was off, too, but she tried to be patient with me since I was working crazy hours on the business and she knew how stressed I was.

More weeks went by, and as my son started sleeping through the night, things were getting easier with the baby. But for me, things started getting worse: I started losing weight. At first it wasn't noticeable, but then I kept on losing weight. I was eating normally but, no matter what I ate and how much I ate, the weight kept coming off.

I was also drinking gallons of water to keep myself hydrated. We lived in the suburbs of Austin, Texas. But as a former New Hampshirite used to the northern climate, the Texas heat was beyond overwhelming. So I kept a 64-ounce Gatorade bottle filled with ice water and drank it constantly. However, something wasn't quite right. Because as soon as it was finished, I'd fill it right back up and drink another. (The unfortunate consequence of this was I'd have to get up five times in the middle of the night to pee.)

I was a mess of thirstiness, fatigue, and weight loss. And for some reason I told myself that my body was stuck in a vicious cycle: I was thirsty all the time because it was hot outside. Because I was thirsty, I was drinking a lot. Because I was drinking a lot, I was getting up to pee multiple times in the middle of the night. And because I was getting up so many times at night, I wasn't getting good sleep. And hence, I was exhausted all the time. To me, it seemed like there was a reasonable explanation for everything.

After the birth of our son, my wife had "encouraged" me to me get life insurance a number of times. Since I hadn't turned 30 yet and I was otherwise in great health, there didn't seem to be any big rush. But because I was the main breadwinner for our now growing family, one day, a few weeks before my 30th birthday, I finally took the time to fill out the application.

After submitting the documentation, a nurse came to our house to do a physical exam and draw blood. She told me I'd learn the results in about three weeks. When she left, I checked "apply for life insurance" off my "to do" list and moved on without a second thought.

In the meantime, I traveled to New York City for work, to attend an industry conference called ClickBank Exchange, and saw some friends from college.

I knew I didn't look good. I had dropped from 165 to 132 pounds (I'm about 5'9"), but I didn't really know *how* bad I looked. Friends I hadn't seen in a while kept saying things like, "Whoa, man. You're pretty skinny. What happened?" I didn't have an answer for them because I didn't know what was going on.

When I returned to Texas, I remember the day like it was yesterday: I walked through my front door and saw a letter from the life-insurance company sitting on the kitchen counter, along with some other mail that had piled up. When I finally got to opening up the life insurance letter, I remember having a strange, uncomfortable feeling in my stomach and my face suddenly getting very hot.

"Denied," it read.

My first thought was that there must be some mistake. They must've sent me someone else's letter. Because after all, I don't smoke, I don't drink, and I just turned 30. I'd never had a major health problem in my life.

So I called my insurance agent to clear things up.

He said, "Ryan, I just got your letter myself. And you might want to sit down. You see, in addition to your letter, I also have your test results in front of me, which I've just emailed you.

Unfortunately, the letter and test results are definitely yours. Now listen, I'm not a doctor, but the levels from your blood work are off the charts." He paused for a moment, "Actually, I've seen this once or twice before. These are textbook Type-1 diabetic numbers," he said. "To me, this looks like juvenile diabetes."

I didn't know what to say. I was 30 years old, and definitely not a juvenile diabetic. Once again, I thought, "There must be some mistake."

But with everything my body was experiencing, part of me worried that it was true.

So I hid the letter, and holed myself up in my office until later that night. My wife finally came in and asked me if the life insurance was taken care of. I showed her my test results and explained what it meant. First, she was silent. Then came the tears.

After we got the baby to bed, she immediately started Googling to find out what my numbers meant. Results pointed to "liver failure," "kidney failure," "pancreatic failure," and even "renal system shutdown."

I still didn't believe the numbers. So my wife rushed to the 24-hour Walmart and returned with every blood-sugar test they had at the pharmacy. A normal reading is about 80 to 100. My wife pricked her finger, and the test revealed that hers was a nearly perfect 85.

My first result? 503. I tested it again: 478. And again: 486.

My heart sank.

Then a wave of panic came over me.

My wife insisted we go to the hospital immediately.

But I was hesitant to go to the ER for a couple of reasons. First, it was practically midnight and it didn't seem like an Emergency Room kind of thing. After all, I wasn't having a heart attack or stroke. Second (and more to the point), I really didn't want to spend the money. We'd just spent a ton on medical expenses with the new baby and with a high-deductible insurance plan; I knew from that experience it was going to cost us another $8,000 just to step through the Emergency Room doors. So I promised my wife that I'd go to the doctor the first thing in the morning. She called the nurse hotline that night, and got us an appointment for the next morning.

When the doctor saw me, heard my symptoms, and looked at my life-insurance lab numbers, he ordered comprehensive blood work done, stat. In fact, he made us stay in the waiting room to wait for the results. After what felt like an eternity and the results came in, the worst of our fears were confirmed.

The doctor took me by the shoulders and looked me right in the eyes.

He said, "Ryan, with these results you should be in a coma. You need to go to the ER *now* and *you* are not driving." I remember my face getting hot—again, just like when I received the life-insurance letter, but this time it felt like I was going to pass out. I heard my wife in the background, starting to cry. "I'd send you in an ambulance but it would actually be quicker for your wife to drive you." My sweet wife pulled herself together and drove me straight to the hospital, knowing that our lives had just taken a detour we never expected.

In the Emergency Room they said I was in a state known as diabetic ketoacidosis, or DKA. DKA can be fatal; my body was shutting down. My sugar levels were extremely elevated and had been for quite some time—possibly months. There was blood in my urine, my kidneys and liver were failing, and my pancreas... well, my pancreas didn't work anymore.

The doctors told me if I had let this go another 24 hours, it's possible I could've died.

They stabilized me and put me into the ICU for nearly a week. My IV was my lifeline. They pumped all sorts of major drugs and nearly 20 pounds worth of fluid to replace all the electrolytes my body had been starved of.

My wife, and the fact that she *insisted* I get life insurance, literally saved my life.

Spending nearly a week in the ICU, even with visiting family and friends, was physically and emotionally isolating. As a father of a newborn baby boy, I found the isolation especially jarring. I missed my family, my friends, and my business. I couldn't do a thing in the ICU.

But as I settled into the intense aloneness, I realized that, for the past few years, I had been so busy with family and creating my businesses that I hadn't taken time to stop and think about what

I truly wanted in life, and what contribution I wanted to make. When you come to terms with your own mortality, it gives you a level of focus and clarity unlike anything else.

I began asking myself questions like, "Okay, you survived this. Now what are you going to do with your life? What do you *want* to do? What kind of *impact* are you going to make?"

My personal process of asking deep questions began.

Now, I may not have known what I wanted, but I definitely knew what I didn't want.

I knew I never wanted to put my family at risk ever again. Although I grew up with a great deal of love, I knew I didn't want my family to feel the same kind of financial stress my parents felt, where money was always tight. I also knew I didn't want to be a slave to a "job" where I was tethered to a Blackberry, commuting for hours, and never seeing my family.

Knowing what I *didn't* want helped me narrow things down. I looked back at my past five years of being in business for myself and I thought, *What were the times in my life that I most enjoyed? What were the experiences and achievements I was most proud of? Where did I make the biggest positive contributions?* There were some consistent trends.

At this point, I had several businesses going at the same time (that I really enjoyed) along with a new baby, so I was pretty busy. I realized that was actually the problem: My focus was way too dispersed. Out of all the things I was doing, I had to pick just one thing to focus on.

After spending days on end in the quiet and stillness of my hospital bed, it hit me like a ton of bricks. And it was there all along. What I enjoy more than *anything else* in business—more than creating products, building supply systems, hiring teams, more than anything—is this:

Figuring out what people want, and giving it to them.

And my unique approach to doing that? The answer was surprisingly simple: applying my *Ask Formula*.

I remember sitting there in the hospital bed; the hair on the back of my neck stood up, and I said to myself, "That's it." I knew exactly what it was. And when I got out of the hospital, I knew exactly what I needed to do.

CHAPTER FIVE

Working Hard for the Dream

When I was a little kid—around ten-years-old—one of my very favorite games was Monopoly. I loved that game. You could buy and sell, make money, and take risks... It took thinking strategically and, if you learned the "ins and outs" and played it right, you could win the game.

It was around that same time my grandparents passed away and left my sister and me each $5,000. It was a huge amount of money for a kid, but my parents said it was mine to do with as I wanted. And what I wanted was... to invest in the stock market.

My parents were great. They got me *The Beardstown Ladies' Common-Sense Investment Guide*, a book by a group of older women who formed an investment club in the 1980s and had gotten great returns. So I read and learned everything I could about the stock market and my folks helped me set up an account to invest it. (For Christmas that year I got Peter Lynch's *One Up On Wall Street*, about the mechanics of investing in the stock market. I couldn't put the book down...)

We lived modestly and my parents both worked full-time (my mom had her own one-woman hair salon and my dad worked for the U.S. Postal Service), but money was always tight. Neither of my parents had gone to college, but they had good jobs and we did a lot of coupon clipping and watched every dime. We certainly didn't go without necessities, but things like going out to eat were rare treats—and we often had to make tough choices on what to forgo.

Growing up I did well in school, but my *real* gift was finding the *shortcuts*. For example, I would regularly convince teachers to let me create videos instead of writing essays, and a buddy and I somehow persuaded our school principal to let us skip fifth grade in favor of building a 12-foot-tall replica of the human body (*all I had to do was take my tests and quizzes, and I was excused from class for the entire year*). I didn't like playing by the rules and regularly tried making my own. As a result, I got good grades but had a reputation for being a bit of a mischievous troublemaker—like the time my best friend and I secretly snuck a car into our high school cafeteria in the middle of the night just to see if we could. Harmless, right?

I excelled in both art and science. But I especially loved science, particularly when it came to the brain. I was fascinated by how the brain works and decided I wanted to get into the best undergraduate program for neuroscience I could, with the hope of becoming a doctor. And so I set my sights on attending the Ivy League school with the best neuro department in the country, Brown University. However, tuition at that time was about $35,000 per year plus living expenses. It didn't matter, because—somehow—I was determined to make it happen.

In high school and every summer during college (except one, when I studied abroad), I worked three jobs. I worked as a grocery store clerk at Shop & Save, I had a landscaping business with my best friend, and he and I were janitors at our high school (his mom was a school principal at the elementary school, so we had an "in"). At $10.00/hr. it was a good-paying job for us kids back then, and I didn't mind the dirty work. The days were long and exhausting. We'd work as janitors during the week, we'd do lawns in the evenings, and then I'd work 10-hour shifts at Shop & Save on the weekends. I saved nearly every penny for college.

Fortunately, I grew up during the roaring 1990s, and by the time I graduated from high school, by making a few smart investments in the semi-conductor industry (and with some luck), I managed to grow the $5,000 inheritance I'd invested as a middle-school student into $85,000 by the time I turned 18—enough to pay for my first two years of college at Brown University.

Even though I made money and was putting away every dime for college, we *still* made nearly every mistake in the book (experience is a great teacher!). For example, we put virtually all the money in my name instead of my parents' name. This turned out to be a terrible decision, because for college financial-aid eligibility, they weigh how much money you have in your name much more heavily than money in your parents' name. So they thought we were rich when I went to college and I got almost no financial assistance.

But I did it. It's not flashy, but that's truly it. I basically worked all through high school mowing lawns, cleaning toilets, and working as a cashier at Shop & Save. My parents invested everything they had in me, and I invested every cent I made to get what I wanted—a shot at attending Brown.

I was committed.

. . .

Needless to say, when I got into Brown, my parents were superproud and happy for me. When I finally got there as a freshman, I randomly sat down next to a kid at lunch on the second day of school and we instantly hit off because we were both into the same thing—neuroscience (yeah, we were those kind of kids).

We went on to become best friends and roommates at Brown.

That kid? He's now Dr. Charles Kassardjian, acclaimed neurologist at the world-renowned Mayo Clinic. We took the same classes and, while things seemed to come easy for him, for me it was always a struggle. Even back then, I knew that, while I loved neuroscience, I would be taking a different path. The problem was, I had no idea which one.

I did know this much: Instead of library research or science experiments, I was interested in practical applications of brain science. Not that I really knew what that meant or what I wanted to do. But I knew I wasn't cut out to focus on one neurotransmitter or one molecule for years and years and have that be the totality of my life's work.

At the same time, I was stoking another kind-of-random passion for East Asian studies and Chinese culture. Now that may seem like quite a jump, but it made sense to me. I was intrigued by traditional Chinese medicine and its impact on the brain. I was also really intrigued by the concept of the brain's ability to learn a foreign language. I had learned French in school growing up (with a name like "Levesque," how could I not?) and loved languages, so Chinese seemed a good match for me.

I really had a thing for Chinese and packed my schedule with as many Chinese-language classes as I could. My grades were good, but I definitely wasn't a natural. I had to work at it, and definitely struggled at times. I realized that if I was ever going to learn Chinese and get *good*, I needed to do something big. I needed to study in China.

So after my sophomore year I decided to enroll in "Chinese Bootcamp" that summer... the single most intense Chinese-language program on the planet. It's an elite program run by Princeton University called *Princeton in Beijing*. It's tough to get into and attracts only the most hardcore people from places like Brown, Harvard, the US Diplomatic Service, and the CIA.

And when I say "bootcamp" I'm *not* exaggerating.

Eight weeks of Chinese, 24 hours a day, seven days a week. Classes start at 6:30 a.m. and end at 10:00 p.m. each night. You eat your meals alongside your teachers. If they hear you reading, writing, speaking ANY English, you're kicked out of the program. No questions asked, no money back.

Or as we'd say, "游戏结束" (yo-SHEE jie-SHU). Translation? Game Over.

But the goal? In eight weeks, you're 100% fluent.

When I started the program, my Chinese was marginal, at best. In fact, I was at the bottom of my group. It's a long story, but I worked my ass off to be the BEST damn Chinese student in that class. I was RELENTLESS. And after eight weeks? I did it. I came back *really* good. I'd done what most people would've considered impossible.

And although my Chinese experience was challenging and rewarding, and I totally loved it—I wondered where it would fit into my plans.

Because in the back of my mind, I still harbored a love for what got me to Brown and *Princeton in Beijing* in the first place: investing in the stock market.

There was something compelling about "highs and lows" of investing. That next summer, between my junior and senior year, I was offered a highly paid summer Analyst position at the Wall

Street gold standard: Goldman Sachs. The pay was almost *triple* what I made working *three* jobs back home in New Hampshire. I've got to admit; there was something really cool about being a college kid working on Wall Street. It was like I was playing Monopoly again; only this time the stakes were higher, the strategies critical, and the money was real money. The experience was challenging and exhilarating and I did my best to rise to the top during my time there. It was exciting, to say the least.

■　■　■

As graduation from Brown drew near, like many other seniors, I was trying to figure out how I could follow both of my passions (Chinese and finance), but I wasn't sure which direction to take.

I had an enviable dilemma: I had two offers from two great companies.

The first offer was from Goldman Sachs. They were offering an amazing package: As a first-year analyst at Goldman Sachs, I would have a base salary and a guaranteed bonus at the end of the year, depending on how well the firm did. That bonus, plus my salary, could add up to a potential $120,000 payday.

When we were in our negotiations, I told them I really wanted to go to China. Their response was, "Sorry, but we only have a rep office in China. Unfortunately, there's really nothing for you to do there." But financially, it was a great offer.

The second offer came through a connection at the big insurance company, American International Group. AIG had ties in China. In fact, AIG had been founded there back in 1919. The connection, Charles Bouloux, was a high-level executive in New York in charge of AIG's Asia Pacific operations, and the company offered me a unique job in AIG's management-training program.

The rub: It paid just a third of what Goldman Sachs was offering, $42,000 with zero bonus.

I accepted.

Everyone said, "Ryan, you're an idiot." (It wasn't going to be the last time I heard those words!)

But the reason I accepted was simple: Charles promised me I would spend a year or two in New York and then the company would send me to China.

I was choosing experience (fulfilling a dream) over money.

I thought: Don't worry. *The money will come later.*

Having accepted AIG's offer, I graduated and put in a call to Charles to let him know I was ready to dive in.

But instead of hearing back from him, I got a phone call from HR.

"I have a little bit of bad news," the woman from HR said. "Charles has had a heart attack. And for health reasons, he's had to step down from his position. But good news, he has a replacement. His replacement is a Brit who ran AIG Europe for the past five years. We've moved him into the Asia-Pacific role. His name is Peter."

CHAPTER SIX

An Unexpected Twist

Life doesn't always go the way we think it will, and mine was no exception.

My new boss, Peter, was now based in New York. And he was *not* expecting to inherit me. The first day we met, he all but said, "I didn't promise you anything. What am I supposed to do with you?"

It was up to me to prove myself all over again.

I ended up working a couple of years at AIG in New York City, my first "real" job. I kept ridiculously long hours, worked in a cubicle, and worked my butt off to prove myself and climb the corporate ladder on Wall Street.

Peter's role (initially that of a direct manager) ended up being one of mentor. He knew I wanted to be in China. But given the tense climate in Chinese relations and internal corporate complications, he sent me to work in Philadelphia of all places as a regional manager for AIG's Global Energy Division.

Not exactly my dream job.

I was living in New York where my then fiancée, Tylene (now my wife), was in grad school. I was commuting three hours a day each way to Philly. So much for using my Chinese.

Then the plot thickened.

I had finally resigned myself to moving to Philly (the commute back and forth to New York was killing me) and the branch I worked at was doing really well. I had sort of committed to the fact that I was going to be there awhile. And then one day, out of the blue, I got a recruiting call by another insurance company: Ace (AIG's number-one direct competitor). Apparently, I had developed something of a reputation in the Philly market. The short story is that Ace offered to double my salary, with a dizzying array of bonuses. And they wanted me right on the spot.

Now, I don't really believe in fate or serendipity, but what happened next was uncanny.

It was a Thursday night, less than 24 hours after getting the job offer from Ace—and I had wrestled with what to do about the decision and talked with Tylene for hours. Together, we decided I would accept the Ace job and give my notice to AIG the next morning.

Then at about 11 p.m. that night, as I was brushing my teeth and getting ready for bed, I got a text message from out of the blue. The name "Peter" popped up. I hadn't heard from him for almost a year. But I'd heard he had left New York for Shanghai to run AIG China and to be closer to the action in Asia.

The message from his Blackberry was just one line and this is what it read:

"Hey, you still want to come to China?"

Now, you have to understand something. At this moment, I was hours away from quitting AIG. If he had sent the text one day later—or even 12 hours later—it's possible the company would've asked me to turn in my company Blackberry immediately after giving notice, which would've meant the message never would've even gotten to me. (And the book you're reading likely never would've been written!)

I texted back immediately: "Are you serious? I'm literally about to take a new job tomorrow morning at Ace. You've got to tell me if this is serious or not." I thought the China opportunity might be a pie-in-the-sky kind of thing, rather than a solid option.

He replied, "It's serious, but I need a little time. Can you buy me a couple of days?" I told him I could give him 48 hours, let him know what Ace was offering, and asked if he could match it.

∎ ∎ ∎

Two days later I heard back: He matched the offer.

I accepted the new position immediately and learned I'd be flying to the Far East in less than 30 days.

It was time to pack up my life and move to China—for real. But, because of Chinese visa restrictions, my fiancée couldn't come unless we were legally married so we had a lightning-quick wedding at Brown, where we'd met. Then, that same week, we packed up everything we owned, put it all into a shipping container to China, boarded a plane, and left immediately for Shanghai.

We moved into our new luxury apartment, housekeeper and all. I got a living stipend—plus a six-figure American salary. I was paid in USD and all my expenses were in Chinese RMB. It was as cushy as it sounds—the ultimate expat lifestyle. There were times when I looked around and thought, "This is it. I've made it." On paper, it was everything I had dreamed it would be, and most people would've killed for the opportunity.

The job expanded rapidly. And after about a year and a half, I started managing a team and opening up sales offices all over China. I traveled constantly, but didn't see much beyond the walls of hotels or my Blackberry screen. My wife had started a PhD program in Hong Kong, so during my rare days off I'd take the two-and-a-half-hour flight there.

But something was off. It was probably around the three-year mark in China when I started feeling discontented and down. "This isn't what it was supposed to be like," I began thinking to myself. I was stressed and lonely. I was building a business, but it was somebody else's business and my efforts felt like I was spitting in the wind. I was running around, managing 20-plus people and spouting Chinese effortlessly. But what was I contributing to the world that was uniquely mine? I thought to myself, "This can't be it."

I basically had a "quarter-life" crisis. I was a wreck. I wasn't even 30 and I was already burning out.

. . .

In the meantime, while I was working like a madman in China, I kept in touch with many of my friends back home, a few of whom were quietly "making money on the Internet." They were doing things on their own terms. A fraternity brother of mine from Brown was making millions playing online poker. And another friend was selling Rave supplies online; he'd tapped into a way to make passive income from his living room, working just a few hours a week. But here's what really got me: these friends from back home weren't any smarter than I was. They didn't work any harder. But they were working on their own terms, making the same kind of money I was making—and a few were making a *lot* more.

On top of the money they were raking in, they weren't spending all their waking hours in airports and hotel rooms like I was. There was something empowering about what they were doing, both literally and figuratively. I began to have this desire to develop something of my own, but I was consumed with *how*.

I emailed my enterprising friends back home and grilled them on exactly from where their successful businesses had sprung. I asked for recommendations—books, courses, the works. On a whim, before an upcoming trip to Malaysia, I decided to download an audiobook with a catchy title: *The Four-Hour Workweek* by Tim Ferriss.

Today it's a well-known book, but isolated in China in 2007, I had never heard of it. While I don't agree with everything in the book, at the time it was a complete paradigm shift for me. And as another Ivy-League graduate who also studied Neuroscience and East Asian studies, Tim's story resonated with me on multiple levels. After listening to the book, I sort of surprised myself when I did something that was so against anything I would have imagined: I ordered a bunch of "how to make money" marketing products off the Internet.

Nobody knew the turmoil going on in my head. To the outside world, I was living a great lifestyle and doing good work. But I felt empty. And the question was: How was I going to explain this bizarre "entrepreneurial" desire to give it all up, and start something from scratch? I knew everyone would think I was crazy.

I didn't know where to turn, so I turned to the one person I thought would understand best. I wrote a super long letter... to my mom.

Now, until I started writing this book, I hadn't let anyone read this letter. It's slightly embarrassing, and deeply personal. But I told a friend about it, he read it, and he convinced me that including it (and not changing a word or a typo) would give a sense of what I was going through and could end up being helpful to other entrepreneurs who may be struggling with finding their right place in the world. I dug it out of my hard drive and read it. Even reading it seven years later brought all those emotions to life again, and I realized what a pivotal moment that was for me.

After a bit of soul-searching (being this open and vulnerable can be a little daunting), I decided to go ahead and include it because it really is "me," warts and all, unscripted and unedited. Every word is true and exactly what I wrote to my mom. But I hope in reading it, it will give you a sense of where I was, and ultimately, the context of how the *Ask Formula* came about.

So here goes...

CHAPTER SEVEN

The Letter

Monday, 8:44 a.m. Shanghai, China

Dear Mom,

As I write to you now, it is quiet in the office. Quickly becoming my favorite time of day. You know, I don't think I'll ever be quite the "natural" morning person that you are (because I do some of my best work at night), but I've been trying to get up a bit earlier every week. I think the benefits of getting up early become more apparent only after making a commitment to yourself to do it. Like many things in life, no one can force you to do it, otherwise it becomes a chore. You have to do it of your own free will. So I've made it a mini-goal of mine to get up 5 minutes earlier every week until I'm consistently getting up at 6:00 a.m. When I get to 6:00, who knows. Maybe I'll keep going.

Anyway, I'm at 6:35 a.m. right now, and I started this little experiment getting up at 7:00 a.m. a few weeks back. I find that not only does it clear my head in the morning to get to the office an hour before the "crowd" comes in, but knowing that I've got a commitment to get up the next morning forces me to be more disciplined with my time throughout the day, and especially in the evening.

Now, I have to say I didn't hit my own target this morning. In fact, I blew it completely. I made it out of bed at exactly 7:16 a.m. (but still made it into the office by 8:04 a.m.—I walk fast), but before I go into that in more detail though, I want to tell you a little something. I'm probably going to ramble a little bit, but it's all going to come together in the end, I promise. So please bear with me.

You see, I'm working on this money-making project, and in fact I have been for a few months now. And when I am really determined to do something (and I mean really and TRULY determined) my focus just completely takes over. Remember when I mentioned something about my focus to you last week? Well this is exactly what I'm talking about. When I am truly focused on a mission, nothing else exists. Every breath from my lungs and every stroke of my hand is made with the singular goal of completing that mission. It's like a force of nature. And right now, that force of nature has taken over.

Let me explain what I mean, by sharing two stories with you from my past, where this force of nature completely took over. You know that when I was younger, most things came pretty easily to me. School, drawing, soccer, piano, etc. I'm not saying that I ever really mastered any of these things, but getting to a certain level of proficiency was pretty easy. But you know how it is, as you get older, the type of things you want to do become tougher and require greater determination. It's easy to say to yourself, "Yeah, I could do that if I wanted," but actually doing it is a different story all together. Well there are two times in my life when I was up against a wall, and when I knew—I just KNEW—that I had to get it done. No matter what it took, I had. To. Get. It. Done. I didn't care if it KILLED me, because I simply was not going to let myself fail.

And let me tell you, looking back, both of these events changed the direction of my life forever. And with age comes more perspective and with more perspective comes wisdom. Now, with this "money-making project" that I'm working on right I feel the same type of life-changing moment about to occur... but first, my stories.

The first story is from junior year of high school.

I still remember my reaction when I got my SAT scores in the mail for the first time. It was like getting kicked in the balls. Since you don't have balls Mom, I'll explain what it feels like. Imagine drinking a bottle of spoiled milk, and then throwing it up, getting punched in the stomach, and crying all at the same time. It doesn't feel good. Anyway, I remember like it was yesterday. I tore open

that letter-sized envelope with great anticipation to learn that...
My score was 1140... hmm. Wait, did I read that right? 1140,
that's it? I read a little further to find out that according to nation-
al statistics, I was barely above "average." To me, this was complete
and utter defeat. This was like God or whoever saying, "Ryan, I
know that you've gotten a bunch of straight A's and everything,
but in the REAL world, this don't mean nothing. You ain't smart.
Who the hell are you trying to kid anyway?"

But I also remember right then and there saying to myself,
"Ryan, the way you handle this situation is going to have an
impact on the rest of your life. Twenty years from now, you will
look back at this very moment, among only a handful of others, as
the few that really and truly shaped your life. And you don't want
to look back and say, 'man I should have just given it a bit more
effort, and maybe just maybe if I did, things would have turned
out differently.'"

So right then and there I decided. I said, "Ryan, it doesn't
matter what it takes, but you've got to do it. I have no idea how,
and don't care if it kills you, but you some how have GOT to get
a 1400 on your SATs."

So as you know, I enrolled in that course at St. A's (of course
you know, you paid for it!) And on the first day of class the
instructor said something to us like, "If you work really REAL-
LY hard, you might be able to get your score up 100 points! In
fact, I've seen it happen once or twice before!" I remember looking around at the other students and they were all floored by that
number. "Impossible!" some of them cried out. But when I heard
that, I had somewhat of a different reaction. I got that same kick-
in-the balls feeling in my stomach again. "That's it?" I thought.
"A measly hundred points?" That sure wasn't going to get the job
done for me. I needed to go up 260 points! But I didn't care what
any instructor said. I knew it was possible. Some how, some way, it
HAD to be possible. So what did I do?

I started to work. And I mean WORK.

You'll of course remember some of this, but every day and
night throughout that summer, I would study. Even at the beach.
In the course of several weeks, I burned through hundreds and

hundreds of verbal and math practice questions. On the verbal side (which was my real weakness) every day I'd force myself to learn new SAT words in groups of 10, until I could recite from memory each word from its definition, and each definition from its corresponding word. I learned over 400 new words like this in just a few weeks.

And soon, I started to see progress.

Every week, on the practice tests my score would go up about 20-40 points (the equivalent of a few extra questions). I soon broke the 1200 barrier. Then 1300. Then 1350. And eventually after two months, 1400. In fact, during one practice exam I scored 780 on the Math section, which meant that I'd only gotten one question wrong in that entire section. I think my all-time high practice test score was around 1440. This was great, but it obviously counted for nothing. I still had to take the test for real.

In the end, I scored 1380 on the real test. 720 math, 660 verbal. Those numbers will be with me forever. It wasn't my personal best, and I didn't quite reach my goal of 1400, but I came damn close. And you know what, I didn't care. The fact was, I had made a 240 point increase in my score, and that was pretty damn good.

But that's not the end of the story.

You see, I'll tell you something else. To me, that test score in and of itself was meaningless. But what it did give me was a chance. A real fighting chance to get into a place like Brown. And I'll tell you what. If it wasn't for that test score, I don't care how many straight A's I had, or how many clubs I belonged to, or how many instruments I played, none of that would have been enough to get me into Brown without that score. You can try to convince me otherwise, but I just know this to be true.

So, if I don't go to Brown, then I don't meet Tylene. I don't meet Tylene, and I don't have the courage to switch from neuroscience to East Asian studies. I don't switch to East Asian studies, and I don't go to China. That test changed my life. And while at the time I had no idea quite how, I just knew with all the fabric of my being that it was going to have a lasting impact on rest of my life.

(Okay, I had to do some work, but I'm back now. It's 12:10 p.m.—lunch time.)

Well, I promised you a second story, so here it is. This one is from the summer after sophomore year of college. At that time, I was really struggling with what I wanted to major in. I came into Brown thinking that I was going to become a doctor, so I studied neuroscience. But you know what I realized at Brown? I didn't want to become a doctor. I took the courses, and slogged through them (got mostly A's and a few B's), but at the end of the day I plain and simply didn't want it. Looking back, I think among a couple reasons, I really wanted the ooh's and ah's you'd get when people would ask you, "So Ryan, what do you do for a living?" It doesn't get much sweeter than being able to say, "I'm a neuroscientist." That is a conversation-stopper. Full stop, end of story. No one else will ever say to that, "Well that's interesting, but I do such-and-such..." It instantly screams out, "I am a genius."

But obviously, that is the wrong reason to want to do anything in life. At least if it's the only reason. I mean, there's nothing wrong with wanting "significance." In fact, most all of us want it in some way or another—whether through love or recognition. But you have to do something because you want it. Because of yourself. If you love what you do, everything else—money, fame, etc. will fall into place. People say that if you want to figure out what you should do with your life, picture that you have ten million dollars in the bank, and don't need another penny. What would you spend your time doing? (I personally think that's a bunch of baloney, because I enjoy making money—it's a way of keeping score with yourself, but I digress...)

Anyway, back to my story.

You see, the problem was, I wasn't quite sure what I wanted to do. And furthermore, I was really afraid that deep down inside, the real reason why I didn't want it (neuroscience, that is), was really because I was afraid I couldn't do it. The classes were tough, I worked a ton with mediocre results, and didn't really enjoy it a whole lot—mostly due to the chemistry and mid-level neuro classes. To put it another way, I was afraid that I was like the "fox and the grapes." If you're not familiar with the story, it's a fable about a fox who jumps and jumps at a bunch of grapes, and after days of doing this unable to catch the grapes, in the end says,

"Those grapes are sour, I didn't want them anyway." That's where we get the phrase, "sour grapes." So at the time, I was afraid I was that fox, even though now I've come to realize that neuroscience simply wasn't what I wanted to devote my life toward.

Whatever. At the same time, I was really enjoying, but struggling with Chinese. My grades were obviously good—all A's, but it masked the fact that Chinese definitely didn't come "naturally" to me like for some of the other kids. I'd often forget how to write basic characters, I wouldn't take chances speaking up in class for fear of messing up, and my pronunciation was horrible.

So at that time, with everything going on, I had sort of lost a bit of confidence in myself. I came to realize that I didn't have what it took (desire + innate intelligence) to someday become a world-class neuroscientist. I was also now starting to appreciate through Brown what it meant to be a tiny fish in an infinitely large pond. But the problem was, I'd already convinced myself that I was supposed to become a doctor. It was my self-outlined "plan." At that time, even one of the janitors at the high school was calling me Dr. Levesque! Deciding to "give up" on neuroscience felt like I was letting everyone down. But more importantly, it felt like I was letting myself down.

So that summer, when I decided to study in Beijing I really needed to prove to myself that I could do something. I mean really DO something. Prove to myself that I still had it in me to do something really amazing. Achievement is one of the greatest motivators in life. And for me, this was SAT time again. I needed that 240 point increase. My goal was simple, I decided to go from being a marginal Chinese student to speaking fluent Chinese, in 8 short weeks. For two whole months, my entire being would be put into this one simple goal even if it killed me.

You have to remember, my self-confidence was still shaky at this point. I'd done everything to pump myself up about being able to succeed. But if there was ever a time in my life where I needed a confidence boost, it was now. The problem is that the program I signed up for—Princeton in Beijing—was not for sissies. It wasn't about "making you feel better about yourself." Anyone who volunteered to put themselves through what is affectionately known as

"Chinese bootcamp" knew that they were really getting them-selves into was actually "Chinese torture." For me, this was exactly what I wanted: The single most intense Chinese-learning experi-ence on the planet, and I was ready to take it by storm.

However, I still had a long way to go before getting there.

You see, on the first day of the program at PIB, this is what happens: Even after you get accepted into the program and you "select" your appropriate Chinese level (first year, second year, etc.), they still make you go to a room with a bunch of other people and take an assessment test to see what your "true" level is. They do this because different schools' Chinese programs move at different speeds. They want to make sure that all students are actually "ready" to be in the class that they've signed up for (in my case, third year Chinese). After they grade the exams, they only call back people who are "on the fence."

I was one of three students called back.

So they get us back in a room and it turns out that the other two students ended up being more advanced than they themselves thought, so they were bumped up to fourth year Chinese. They were then asked to leave the room, and that left only me. At that time, the PIB people basically told me that according to my assess-ment test, I was on the fence between the second and third year program, so they wanted to ask me some questions verbally in Chinese.

Now at this point, remember that feeling I had when I opened up my SAT scores in the mail for the first time. Well this was anoth-er "kick-in-the-balls" moment for me, but this time compounded with sudden fear and anxiety.

Being dropped down to second-year Chinese would be devas-tating. It would be remedial. It will kill all hopes of advancement. To put it in perspective, there were three other students from Brown who each only had one year of Chinese under their belts, and they were all in the second-year program. I personally already had two years of Chinese, which was one whole year more than them. So being dropped down would have essentially meant that my Chinese was no better then theirs. Or basically, that I'd wasted an entire year studying Chinese at Brown.

Fortunately for me (and my ego) I passed their verbal test, but nevertheless, being the only student "on the fence" in the third-year class deeply imprinted a very clear and distinct message in my brain:

I was the worst student in the whole entire class.

But...

You have no idea what a blessing this turned out to be for me! You see, it motivated the HELL out of me. I wasn't going to let anyone tell me I didn't deserve to be in that third year class. In fact, the experience even caused me to revise my goal: I would go from being the absolute worst stinking miserable excuse for a student in that class, to becoming the #1 absolute best, in a matter of 8 weeks (even if it killed me).

So like with the SAT prep. I started to work. And I mean WORK.

Every single day, it was nothing but Chinese for me. Especially during the first four weeks. I wrote up flash cards for every single word that I needed to learn. After class was over, I would copy over and over again all the characters I'd learned, 20 times each. I only took two breaks a day—to eat lunch and dinner. Teachers held office hours at 10:00 p.m. and I was there every night. Up at 6:00 a.m. in bed by 12:00 a.m. Nothing but Chinese, day in and day out. The program was designed like that, but like most things in life, you get out what you put in. And I'll tell you, I don't think there was a single person in the program that worked as hard as I did. Best of all, I loved it.

I immediately started seeing returns on my investment. I started speaking up in class. I'd study 200 new words a day, (I'd only remember 50, but what the hell! 50 words x 5 days x 8 weeks would make 2000 words!—which just happens to be the exact number of words people say is the threshold of fluency in Chinese), and my vocabulary was expanding at an exponential rate.

Oh, I almost forgot to mention. All the while during PIB, I remember having SYMS in the back of my mind. Do you remember that program? Yeah, the summer music school that I did between 8th grade and high school. It was WAY over my head. I simply couldn't handle it. I wanted to go home, and I absolutely hated it. I cried when you guys visited, blah blah blah. Well anyway, that was first time in my life, I realized that I was a not-so-big fish, in even just a medium-sized pond. But it also taught me that I NEVER wanted to go through an experience like that again. I never ever wanted to publicly feel like such a failure. It's worked both ways for me in my life so far—it's motivated me to always prepare to the fullest, but it's also made me deathly afraid of public failure, which has held me back from taking some of really biggest chances in life, but I'll get into that some other time.

Anyway, back to the story.

After building what I considered to be my own personal bullet-proof Chinese study system (a.k.a. work like a dog), do you know what happened then?

I started getting really good. And I mean, REALLY good. I definitely wasn't perfect, and I was probably my own biggest critic, but I took advantage of every single tiny drop of Chinese knowledge that I could from every class, every individual session, every office hour that I attended. I sucked them PIB teachers dry!

How did it all turn out? Well, I've got to be honest and say that I didn't become the #1 best student in my class after the 8 weeks. In fact, I probably wasn't even in the top 5. But you know what? I didn't care. I proved to myself that I could do it. I could improve my Chinese to the stratosphere, under the right conditions, through hard work and determination alone. Now if you're wondering about the results, I think the best way to describe my transformation over those 8 weeks is through another story.

Remember, I was a marginal Chinese student (at best) at Brown before going into PIB. Now, after the program I skipped from second to fourth year Chinese (which is typical), and on the first day of class the Professor (who was also incidentally my first-year Chinese teacher as well), asked a few students, "How was your summer? What did you do? Etc."

Well, when she finally came around to asking me, as soon as the first sentence came out of my mouth...

Her jaw literally hit the floor.

I'm telling you: Hit. The. floor. She didn't say a word. She just stood there. It was just silence for about 10 seconds. That moment will be with me for the rest of my life. Right then and there, without saying a word she told me what I wanted to know. As far as learning Chinese was concerned, I had done the impossible.

After the initial shock wore off, she just started asking me a bunch of rapid-fire questions with really tough vocabulary, and no one else in the class knew what the hell we were saying. In fact, after we were through, no other student wanted to even open their mouth!

While I obviously never claimed this to anyone or gave off the impression that I felt this way, between you and me, I was the best student in that class—by a mile! So to summarize, in May 2002 I was (at best) a marginal second-year Chinese student. And by August 2002—three months later, I had jumped to becoming the best fourth year Chinese student in the entire school. Fast forward to today and here I am living half-way across the world in China fooling Chinese people every day that I'm some Chinese-caucasian freak of nature. Anything is possible.

(It's 3:06 p.m. now, and I've been going back and forth between this letter and some work tasks)

By now, (if you haven't already) you're probably wondering why the hell I'm writing all this. You might even be a bit concerned. Don't be. Everything is perfectly fine. In fact, I'm writing because I am so overwhelmed with enthusiasm right now that I have to just get it all out on paper. This is probably the longest letter I've ever written. Maybe the longest one you've ever read.

You see, the two stories that I just told changed me as a person forever. Maybe they don't seem like a big deal to you, maybe they do. The fact is, these were two situations where I grabbed life by the shoulders and said, you know what? No. Don't tell me this can't be done. I don't care what it takes. I WILL do this.

Sure I came out of those experiences with more knowledge. But that's not the point. The point is, I said to myself that I was going to do something that would take an extraordinary amount of hard work, with a good chance I'd fail (if you read my stories again, I actually "failed" both times!), and for some reason it gave me the confidence to take on the world.

The problem is though, I haven't really had any experiences like those for some time now. Not that life-changing at least. Maybe not even since college graduation. You see, for me graduation was like sophomore year all over again. I wasn't really sure what I wanted to do. My major goal was to work in China, and get paid good money doing it, and that was about it. And now, I've done that. I grossed about $140K last year (unfortunately with lots of taxes—technically $189K+ if you include the tax equalization AIG gives me, but I never see a dime of that money), and now have $120K+ invested for our retirement. I'm proud of both those things. And it never would have been possible without the loving support of Tylene and you and Dad and Allie throughout the whole journey. But here's what's been bugging me: Right now, I'm doing my "dream job." This is what I set out to do the day I joined AIG, and it's taken me almost 4 years to get here. And now that I'm here, you know what I'm saying to myself?

I'm saying, "This is it?"

Some people say that in life you have to enjoy the journey, not the destination. The journey to where I am today has been awesome... Although, when I look myself in the mirror, there's a nagging feeling of knowing that I had more to give. I didn't take enough risks, and I could have done so much more. And when it comes down to it, I don't want the next 4 years to blow by the same way.

In all honesty, I worked hard a few times these past few years at AIG, but mostly I was gliding by. When I really dissect it, my real success can be boiled down to one thing. I was able to make myself extremely valuable in the eyes of one single man, Peter. Everything else has been secondary. Now there's nothing necessarily wrong with that, but that's not how I want to live my life—with someone else as my master. I am my own master. But I'll get into that a little bit later.

For now, let me tell you a story about soccer. When I look back at my soccer career, there is only one game in my life that I can honestly say if there was a gun to my head, I literally could not have played any harder—even if my life depended on it.

It was my last game of the season, senior year of high school. We were the #12 seed playing the #1 seed, Hanover, and we were playing on their field. We barely squeaked into the play-offs, and they were undefeated that year. I remember thinking to myself, "Ryan, this might be the last time that you ever play a real competitive soccer game for the rest of your life. Play like it will be." Well, we lost that game 1-0. But they didn't score on us until something like the 85th minute of the game, and we dominated those first 85 minutes. I mean DOMINATED. Ask Dad. He'll remember. I played forward for the entire game. No breaks. And I ran my heart out. You may remember some other games that I played hard, but I'm telling you there was never anything like this game for me, ever. I was in a completely different state of mind. For me, it was like the World Cup finals, and by the end of it, I couldn't even walk. I couldn't even stand up. I just collapsed on the center circle. We didn't win. I didn't even score. But nearly 10 years later that is the most memorable game in my entire soccer career.

Right here, right now I am making a commitment to myself to live the rest of my life like that game.

Leave nothing on the field.

You see, here's what I'm getting at with all this.

At a place like AIG, it's easy to get complacent. The benefits are good, the pay is decent, and all the "little things" are taken care of. You say to yourself, yeah it's not what I imagined, but I could spend the rest of my life doing this. I guess. But there's a nagging. Something that's not quite right. Not quite complete. It comes and it goes, but it never goes away. If you come into a place like this with a fire in your belly, well they just blow that fire out. Slowly, over time. In fact, you don't even really notice it happening to you.

Every additional year you stick around, it gets harder and harder to leave. And when I say leave, I'm not only talking about leaving AIG, I'm talking about leaving the cushiness of ANY big company. Once you get fully dependent on the safety net that a company offers, that lifestyle, you're dead in the water. They've got you for life, and there ain't nothing you can do about it.

You see, there's a big price that you've got to pay for that safety net. And that price is control. When you work at a company like say an AIG, they control when you work, where you work, how much they want to pay you, and what kind of work you want to do. I mean really, AIG isn't the big bad wolf. Any company is like that. Sure, you can always stand at the knees of your boss and beg for more money (a.k.a. ask for a raise), but who likes to beg?

When you're in business for yourself, you control when you want to work: 5 day marathon sessions, then a month off? Sure! Where you work: Let's spend half the year in Asia, and then half the year in Europe! How much you want to pay yourself: You want more money? Well, that's up to you to crack that nut. What kind of work you want to do: Anything that the blob of grey matter between your ears can come up with.

So here's what I'm getting at:

Right here, right now I am making a commitment to myself to take back control.

And if I could add to that a bit, someone famous once said that there's no greater satisfaction for man, than to be self-reliant. And for me, this is what it all comes down to. Control and self-reliance.

Fortunately for me, the fire in my belly that I had when I graduated Brown still has a little flicker left to it. And a few weeks ago, it was re-ignited. In an instant, it was like I was reborn.

I've had this feeling nagging at me ever since graduation, the feeling of wanting to do my own thing, get my own company off the ground. I've made some small attempts to break loose of the corporate choke-hold, but these were feeble and half-hearted at best. Back in New York in 2005, for example, I met a guy at AIG who had started his own company with his wife on the side. He and I got together for a little while. It didn't work out. In the end, it was his thing, and I wanted my thing. We're still friends today. Last year, when I was a bit down in the dumps at work (when things were slow), I was thinking about doing something with art. I wasn't quite sure what, but again...that idea fizzled. As Tylene knows, over the past 4 years I've done an awful lot of talking, but not a whole lot of doing. And then, like a ton of bricks, it hit me in the face one day about a month ago.

Just shut the hell up, and do it.

So that's where I am today. Actually, that's where I was about 3 weeks ago, and I'm getting this all down on paper for the first time. It dawned on me, that every major success in my life—the things that were "impossible"—occurred because I just shut up and did it.

And that's what I'm doing this time—with a sense of urgency that I've never felt before. It's like a lighting bolt running down my spine. Why now? Well, for some crazy reason, it just occurred to me the other day that I'm not going to live forever. I could get hit by a bus tomorrow. So if not now, it could be never.

So right here today, I am making three promises to myself.

I will focus on this like when I raised my SAT score 240 points.

I will discipline myself to make progress every day, no matter how small, like I did when I learned Chinese at PIB.

I will live every day of my life with a sense of urgency like that game up in Hanover.

I'm going to have to work like a bastard for this. No one needs to tell me that. But why the hell not? If it kills me, then it kills me. But it won't. If I fail, then who the hell cares. My proudest achievements in life were all failures! I must be screwed up.

If you're wondering if I'm going to quit AIG, the answer is no. At least not just yet. But I'm now working on an exit strategy with the shortest timeframe possible. If you're wondering if I've lost my mind, the answer is also no. I'm just pouring this all down on paper, to help clear things in my head. You see,

This is my personal manifesto.

And why am I sending it to you? Because Mom, you're probably the only person in the whole wide world that loves me enough to read the whole damn thing. But you have to promise me this. You have to keep this secret. I also don't want to talk about it, unless I bring it up. So you have to promise me not to ask me about it.

Tylene knows all the details of what I'm working on, so don't worry. It's nothing illegal. It's good old-fashion business. It's also low risk, and won't require me to bet my life savings, anything close to that, or do anything crazy in general (except work like a madman). At the end of the day, it's just going to take tons and tons of good old-fashioned hard work, and you know what? One day it's going to make me stinking rich. And when that day comes, it will be the whole family's to share.

I just don't want the whole world or whole family to know what's going on quite just yet. So can you promise to keep it under wraps? I'll know when the time is right, and I'll be the one to share with everyone then. I share more details when I've got news that's worth sharing.

Until that time, just know that your son is going to be working some O.T. Basically the equivalent of two full-time jobs, probably more. This is going to be the most difficult thing that I've ever attempted, and I'd be lying if I said that I wasn't just a little bit scared. But I know that if its been done before (and it has), then there's no reason on earth why I can't do it either. Who knows, this might be my greatest "failure" yet, but one thing's for certain. The time is now. So as they say,

"Ladies and gentlemen, buckle your safety belts, because this is going to be one hell of a ride."

I love you,
Ryan
—April 28, 2008 (8:02 p.m.)

■ ■ ■

After writing this letter to my mom, I *had* to make this work. After all, I'd promised her I wouldn't give up. I was working hard and getting pats on the back at AIG, setting up all those new offices, but my heart wasn't in it. I was far from being fired, but what I wanted was to be on fire. I wasn't okay with burning out.

CHAPTER EIGHT

Standing on the Shoulders of Giants

The books, courses, and entrepreneurial tools I had ordered started arriving in China.

People shared their strategies for (mostly) online success. Some approaches were complete BS, while others were kind of interesting.

But there was one particular course that stood out: the writings of (the late) Gary Halbert. Regarded as one of the top copywriters in the world, he had a striking style that intrigued me.

While I had been taught to write academically using big SAT words and trying to impress Ivy League professors with long sentences, Halbert used short sentences and short words that packed a big punch. His writing style lingered in my brain.

I had read somewhere that a really great copywriter would never go hungry—if you learn how to write words that move people and persuade them to buy, that skill will never go out of fashion.

That made sense. So I decided to invest time in developing that skill, and *The Gary Halbert Letters* was my first introduction to the world of direct-response copywriting.

Halbert had put an archive of his (normally, very expensive) work, including 25 years of marketing newsletters, online for free. I decided to study this newsletter like crazy. It gave me an education—not just in what he was saying, but the way he was saying it.

I knew there was a correlation between learning using longhand (vs. typing) and was so intrigued by his compelling style that I started copying his newsletters word for word in longhand in composition notebooks—no small feat. Because my wife was in Hong Kong pursuing her PhD, I'd come home to an empty apartment at night and on the weekends. I basically spent every waking moment studying copywriting and writing out these over-the-top compelling letters by hand.

This was my "normal" routine for about five months. I'd come home from work at 6:00 in the evening. In Asia, they have McDonald's delivery guys on scooters and let's just say I was a great customer. Every night I'd eat hamburgers and copy Halbert's writing word for word. I immersed myself in copywriting (I knew that's what it would take, like when I immersed myself in Chinese one summer in college). Over time, I knew it was sinking in. As I copied these 10-page newsletters, I felt the language getting etched into my brain with every stroke of my pen and bite of French fries.

The content of his newsletters wasn't what I was focused on. They might have described promotions Halbert was running or giving lessons in building business. But the way he wrote... genius.

I quickly realized that no matter what your vocabulary or verbal ability, no one likes being talked down to. Unless you live in the world of academia (where verbal one-upmanship is the norm), most people prefer common, everyday conversation.

The important part of what I was learning was his style of communicating. The magic was in the way he wrote. Something about it inspired passion, and stoked that flame inside me. I knew I was on to something, and so I kept copying.

The thing I (still) love most about Gary Halbert's style of writing is that it makes you feel like he's talking to you in your living room, just having a casual conversation. His words stuck. I had to "unlearn" an academic/corporate style of writing I'd picked up in college and been praised for in the corporate world.

But eventually, I began writing my own copy, and it began to take on life, color, and personality. I wrote to connect with people. My intent was to never, ever to be disrespectful but to help the reader feel connected. Like Halbert, I learned to write to one person—a person with needs and desires just like me.

In time it clicked: I was moving from being a corporate businessman, working for a big company, feeling unsatisfied and empty, to learning how to communicate and sell in a powerful kind of way.

∎ ∎ ∎

"When the Student is Ready, the Teacher Will Appear..." This was certainly true for me.

Now that I knew I had a writing style that was comfortable and compelling, my big entrepreneurial question was, "What business do I want to start?"

It was then that I heard a podcast of an interview with a man named Dr. Glenn Livingston. It caught my attention on how to choose the right market.

I had looked at the world around me in Shanghai, trying to figure out what I wanted to do (I even looked around the contents of my apartment for inspiration) and came up with lots of potential answers... but still, I was blank.

The interview with Dr. Livingston gave me some ideas, but I knew I needed more. His podcast was helpful but also intended to sell a product: a 25-page PDF on how to choose your market. It was selling for $17.

Clear as day, I remember how my finger hovered over the mouse button, ready to click "Complete Order Now." I went back and forth; to buy or not to buy?

I thought, *$17 bucks? Screw it. Just DO it!*

(Later those words would be repeated—and today, I consider them the "five most profitable words of my career." That's a story for another day...)

For a moment, I felt this wave of remorse... because, even though it was only 17 bucks, I'd gotten the distinct impression, as I researched books and videos on how to start businesses and be successful, that lots people advising on this were basically scam artists.

A lot of products I got sounded good—but these people had never actually started businesses themselves—beyond the business of selling their own stuff on "how to start businesses." They were teachers, first and foremost: good at getting people to buy what they were teaching—but that was pretty much it.

There was a seeming contradiction in real-world application and proven success, and I didn't trust them.

But when I heard Glenn Livingston, I sensed immediately that he was totally different.

He had a distinct methodology, which he'd used to get into lots of small niche markets. He had sold eBooks on how to care for your guinea pig, how to care for your pygmy goats, how to raise an alpaca farm... and how to detect radon in your home. None of them were huge markets, but they all made a couple thousand dollars every month—adding up to something like $30,000 of monthly income for him. Not too shabby.

The reason why he launched his slew of small businesses? Surprisingly, it all stemmed from a major international disaster—9/11.

With his wife, Livingston had developed this crazy-expensive multi-million-dollar conference center in New York. They'd poured their life savings into this project—and then launched right before the Twin Towers were attacked, and lost everything in the aftermath. He even went $2 million into debt, and became so risk-averse that he resorted to only working on projects that wouldn't lose a ton of money in one fell swoop. His discovery: lots of tiny markets.

In financial parlance, he diversified his risk.

Beyond his academic and corporate prowess, there was another connection that drew me to Glenn. After he lost money in New York, he wanted to get away from it all—so he moved with his wife to my home state of New Hampshire, about 15 minutes from where my parents still lived. I had even driven down the street he wrote about when I was growing up. What were the chances?

Finally, and most compellingly, I liked that his market selection strategy was all about the numbers. A "Livingston-style" approach to selecting a market might go something like...

"If a market has X number of Google searches every single month, and there are Y number of competitors, and the click prices on Google AdWords are in the reasonable range, then it's a contender."

Livingston explained exactly how to look at metrics to choose the size of a market to enter. For instance, if a market had too few people searching for a solution on Google, then it might not be worth bothering with, while a market with high search volume could be too competitive. He gave specific advice on which markets to choose and how, based on the success he'd found in the tiniest and most random of niche markets.

After buying that first $17 product—and deciding he wasn't a scam artist—I started purchasing everything Glenn had to offer.

Including the $2,000 course that explained his whole system, from start to finish—which, at the time, was more money than I'd ever spent on anything online, by a considerable margin.

A week or two later, the package arrived in China. It was a box filled with binders, DVDs, CDs... and the box was completely busted. The CD and DVD cases were all cracked. The binders and books had been hit with serious water damage. But miraculously enough, the DVDs worked. And that first weekend, I was so excited to dive in—I watched the whole thing...

All 20 hours.

The method was full of advanced statistical concepts. It was esoteric. It involved things like "cluster analysis" using tools like the statistical software SPSS. The analytical geek in me totally lit up. His style couldn't have been further from Gary Halbert's... but it spoke to me. I was, after all, a bit of a geek deep down—and so was unfazed by the dense numbers-speak.

It was a good thing that DVD didn't get scratched or broken like almost everything else in the package it came in, because what was contained in that package literally changed my life.

Glenn Livingston's approach helped me focus on what mattered most: the market. I realized that it was much easier to find a market and figure out what to sell them than to have a product and have to create a market for it.

Soon I would launch my first business following his advice. Later on, my success would snowball, I'd build my own methodology (using his as a jumping-off point)... and we'd become great friends. I wouldn't be where I am now if I hadn't found him.

Before those 20 hours, I had my sales language down pat, but had no idea what to sell or how to sell it. But after watching it repeatedly—soaking up the dense information—I now had a plan. I knew how to carry out my market research, settle on a market, and figure out what that market really wanted.

As a fairly new entrepreneur, I was hungry for big-time success. But I wasn't a big risk-taker; in fact, I had always been relatively risk-averse about losing money.

Was success in entrepreneurship totally about being in the right place at the right time? That wasn't my style. I wanted a formula.

CHAPTER NINE

Taking the Leap

Sometimes great things are created from the most unexpected and unlikely places.

That couldn't be more true of my first business, which would end up laying the groundwork for my *Ask Formula* methodology.

The unlikely place? A small but growing craft site called Etsy.

Etsy.com is "a place to buy and sell all things handmade." In the pre-Internet "old days," arts-and-crafters typically sold their wares in open-air markets. Etsy was created in 2005 as a global online "craft fair," giving sellers personal storefronts where they listed and sold their goods for a small fee. (They are now generating over a billion dollars in total annual transactions.)

We were still living in Asia at the time, and my wife, Tylene, who was into crafts, loved the site. Etsy attracted mainly women and was getting phenomenal growth and traffic. (Etsy sellers range from hobbyists to professional artists, and most sellers are women who tend to be college-educated and in their twenties and thirties.)

At the time, one of the more popular items sold by a number of crafters on the site was jewelry made from Scrabble® tiles. On Etsy.com, you could look at any individual seller's sales history, organize those sales by date, and see how many sales of each product they were making each day. In this Scrabble-tile jewelry market, we could see that there was good money to be made.

But when it came to creating product, neither of us wanted to get into creating individual pieces of jewelry—or, for that matter, employing Chinese workers to do it. But there were one or two sellers who had taken a slightly different path. Not only were they

51

selling the jewelry itself, they were also selling guides on how to make the jewelry as well.

Despite selling dozens of copies each day, these guides weren't very well done. We knew this firsthand, because we tried learning how to make the jewelry ourselves using these guides. Unfortunately, these guides were incomplete. They created more questions than answers. Eventually, we were able to figure out how to make the jewelry on our own. It required putting together a number of missing pieces that weren't explained anywhere—except through intense trial and error.

So we thought, "What if we build a better mousetrap?" We decided to create the best Scrabble-tile jewelry-making tutorial guide available on the market, period.

Our early results were underwhelming. Initially, it was like launching to crickets. After all, we had no sales history. No reviews. People didn't know or trust us. So to get things going, we had to hustle. We offered heavy discounts. We reached out to people directly in online forums. Eventually we got some traction, and after getting our first few critical sales, a handful of rave reviews and learning the ins and outs of selling on Etsy, sales started to pick up.

But there was a problem: We started getting questions.

When it came to making the jewelry, people kept running into the same handful of challenges.

For example, people would tell us, "This is great, but the paper I'm using makes the ink run. What should I do?" or "How do you treat a photograph differently than a piece of porous origami paper?" or "What if I want to use glass-mosaic tiles instead of Scrabble tiles?"

I realized, like everybody else selling Scrabble-tile-jewelry instructional guides, we were treating the market as one homogenous group. But really, there were three distinct "buckets" of people:

1. People who wanted to make Scrabble-tile jewelry using origami paper.
2. People who wanted to make photo jewelry using Scrabble tiles.
3. People who want to make glass-mosaic-tile jewelry using a similar, but slightly different process.

All required nuanced (but important) tweaks to the main process, and we realized the "one-size-fits-all" guide didn't really address any one of these subgroups very well.

So we asked ourselves, *What if we create separate guides for each of these three "buckets" of people and then sell them individually—and as a discounted bundle for people who want to learn it all?*

That's when we hit pay dirt. When we created multiple, customized products like this for each of the three major segments of the market, we became the number-one player practically overnight. We went from barely making $500 per month to making over $10,000 per month between our website and Etsy shop. And we did it in a tiny, obscure niche. Furthermore, since our guides were more "specialized," and more directly addressed people's specific questions, we were able to charge premium prices. While the generic, one-size-fits-all guides our competition produced sold, on average, for $9.00, we sold our "specialty guides" for $17.00 each and the bundle of three for $33.00.

And the best part? Our customers LOVED what we produced.

And that was when the "aha moment" came. We discovered that by paying attention to the right information, you could not only identify what sub-segments exist in your market, but you can also identify *which ones are worth focusing on*. And when you've done that, you can determine which products to sell, and how to customize your marketing language to speak to each of those segments' wants, needs, and desires—differently. I didn't realize it at the time, but looking back, it was then that the seeds of the *Ask Formula* began to sprout.

. . .

It was after paying attention to what the market was asking that I began to shift my thinking. I started to realize that the real power came in *integration of a few key ideas*. The parts of the puzzle were beginning to come together. Things began to work when I combined good old-fashioned, on-the-street salesmanship with a sophisticated, statistically based model of survey questions to get feedback from our customers.

If you only have one element and not the other, you're off-balance and ineffective. If you only use "door-to-door" salesmanship without substance and structure behind it, then all you've got is a huckster model. If you only apply a heady, sophisticated model with academic language, you lack connection with your customer.

I starting seeing positive results and results, as I discovered later, that were repeatable. I knew I was connecting. I had learned to speak, write, and communicate in a way that just about anyone can relate to, from grocery-store clerk to the PhD-level economist—with both of them feeling like I was talking directly to them. At the same time, I was laying down the structure and design so the process could be analyzed, refined, and repeated.

This combination, more than anything else, is responsible for why this model was starting to get incredible, and as I was about to soon learn, *repeatable* results.

It was time to go full-throttle and see what happened.

■ ■ ■

Now that my entrepreneurial flame was really getting fanned, I set my sights on leaving behind the corporate job that was taking its toll on the both of us. I was tired of traveling all the time and missing my wife.

And then a devastating thing happened that actually turned out to be a good—no, a great—thing. Rumors start flying around that AIG was in financial trouble. It was complicated, but a division of AIG was somehow involved in the same global financial crisis that brought down Bear Stearns and Lehman Brothers. And then, one day, it all came to a head when I stepped into my office to see the *Wall Street Journal* Asia edition read "AIG to File for Bankruptcy." When I read that headline, I decided it was now or never. It was time to go for it. Time to go into business for myself, never work for anyone else again, and never look back.

I gave AIG my notice, donated everything I owned except for what could fit in two suitcases, and moved to Hong Kong, where I was finally back with my wife.

Since she was a graduate student, her accommodations weren't exactly the luxury lifestyle I had gotten used to in Shanghai. She had a $500 monthly stipend and lived in a 400-square-foot apartment—now split between us.

My retirement money was all tied up and I had put away a little cash for emergencies, but my expense account and paycheck were gone. Armed with nothing but a $400 Gateway laptop, I spent every waking moment working to build my fledgling business, spending as little money as possible on a daily basis.

But almost as soon as our Scrabble-tile jewelry Etsy empire began to take off, the market for Scrabble-tile jewelry crashed. Like Beanie Babies, pogs, and so many other trending markets, the Scrabble-tile craze was a just passing fad. The market had disappeared almost overnight. And there we were, back to square one again. But this time, there was no safety net of a cushy six-figure salary. My back was up against a wall, and I needed to figure something out—fast.

CHAPTER TEN

Things Finally Come Together

Shortly after the "Great Scrabble-Tile Jewelry Crash of 2008," and while we were still living in Hong Kong, my wife, who had always been incredibly supportive when I was making big changes, unexpectedly received an amazing job offer to become a museum curator in south Texas (which also happened to be where her family lived) at the Brownsville Historical Association.

The timing could not have been better. We needed a source of income, but more importantly, this was an amazing job opportunity for her and, after all she had done for me, I felt like it was her turn. Since my work was mostly done from my laptop, there was no reason to stay in China. It was time to move to Texas.

We wanted to live somewhere near her work and be relatively close to her family. The border city of Brownsville, Texas, while historically important, is possibly most well known today for having one of the poorest zip codes in the country.

Our financial situation was pretty much the same as it was when Tylene was a graduate student. We both agreed it was better to live simply so we could put every spare dollar into the business. While the Scrabble-tile jewelry market had crashed and basically put us back to square one, we'd gotten a taste for success—and, most importantly, confidence in our approach.

When we came back to the U.S., we owned next to nothing, and were basically starting from scratch. Fortunately, we didn't require much. We splurged on a $200 mattress and found a $5 TV with a crooked set of rabbit ears that we bought off Craigslist We hit it big when we got two collapsible lawn chairs as a "free gift" (which became our "living room furniture") when we opened our U.S. corporate bank account (It was a good thing they didn't require a big deposit to get the free gift!)

We spent $50 a week on groceries at the local Walmart, never bought new clothes, and just totally focused on work. For big excitement, once a week we splurged on a date at a local drive-in fast-food joint called Stars, which served $1 hamburgers on Thursdays. We'd get three, and split them.

The only thing I spent money on was high-speed Internet access.

. . .

Sometimes starting over at the bottom can be the best thing you can do for yourself.

This bare-bones lifestyle put productive pressure on me to create a business and make it profitable fast. I knew myself, and I knew I needed a sense of urgency to make things happen. Living on one salary (Tylene's museum curator's salary in Brownsville was $36,000/year) challenged me to do my best, do it well, and do it *fast*. I made a conscious choice not to dip into our retirement or emergency funds, and there really weren't any other options. I had to make it work.

But here's how I played out the downside risk: I had a "mental safety net." By living with practically nothing and keeping our expenses as low as possible, it helped me overcome the fear of failure. If things didn't work out, I knew what the worst-case scenario looked like. And if push came to shove, I'd go out and get a job, save a little money, and start back up again. I was fortunate enough to have a wife (my partner) who supported that vision.

The good news was it never came to that. All that diligence, commitment, and sacrifice paid off. It didn't take long for us to start making money again, and eventually, make it big.

. . .

After our rollercoaster experience in the Scrabble-tile jewelry market, I decided to launch a second business—this time in an *evergreen* market, without the risk of it being a short-term fad. I decided to pick a sub-niche within the most popular hobby markets of all time: gardening.

I consider it our first "real" Internet business, because it's one we grew from $0 to $25,000 per month within 18 months, and eventually to nearly half-a-million dollars per year. It's also the first business in which I first used the *Ask Formula* in its "modern" form.

From there, I had ambitions to launch my first seven-figure business, and decided to use the *Ask Formula* to enter the memory-improvement market. We eventually went on to create a business and brand called RocketMemory™, which went on to become arguably my most well-known, and certainly most successful, niche business. Through mastermind groups with other entrepreneurs, this business started drawing interest and attention from people who wanted me to do what I had done for *my* businesses—successfully apply the *Ask Formula*—in their businesses.

In fact, this led to a massive shift in our business model. Our focus on teaching and working directly with other companies to apply the *Ask Formula*—which my team and I have now done in market after market—generating tens of millions of dollars in the process.

But it was through those early ventures, armed with Halbert's copywriting lessons and Livingston's wise words about market selection, that I began to very quickly understand what questions to ask potential customers, how to frame these questions, and what to do with the results. With lots of trial and error and a steep learning curve, I've fine-tuned a system, a formula if you will, for getting the questions right every time.

And in this book, I'm going to hand that formula to you on a silver platter.

■　■　■

Fast forward to 2012. Things were going well. The niche businesses generated far more passive income than we needed to sustain our lifestyle. And because they didn't require my day-to-day involvement, I was free to pursue multiple side projects, run a growing consulting practice, and make time for the increasing number of people who wanted to work with my growing team and me to apply the *Ask Formula* in their businesses.

We had a new baby, and life was good.

That is, until I ended up in the ICU.

But out of that awful situation came incredible *focus*. And from that focus I discovered what I was most passionate about: helping other business owners reach their financial goals and have happy customers coming back for more. After leaving the hospital, I started divesting myself of all the side projects, clients, and businesses I was involved in that weren't singularly focused on this one thing: applying the *Ask Formula* in market after market.

Today, that's what I do, all day, every day. I advise and coach business owners through the process of applying the *Ask Formula*. I run online training programs and in-person mastermind groups for business owners looking to use *Ask Formula* to take their business to the next level. I even own a marketing agency that does all the implementation work for businesses that want the entire process done for them.

In the following chapters, I'm going to give you everything you need to apply the *Ask Formula* to your business—and when we're finished, I'm going to explain the reason why I've decided to give my entire formula away like this. As for the *Ask Formula* itself, some of it is a bit technical, so stay with me. I'll take you through every step.

The question is: Are you ready?

Part II

ASK:
THE METHODOLOGY

CHAPTER ELEVEN

Getting Started

How to Read the Ask Formula *Methodology*

Now that you've arrived at the Methodology section of the *Ask Formula*, I want to give you some parameters and a bit of a roadmap to reading.

While it's true that some people cringe a little when starting to read the "nuts and bolts" of how to put something like this into action, I have to tell you, I get pretty excited because this is where the "rubber meets the road." Once you understand how the *Ask Formula* works and apply it to your business, if you're like most people, it will become one of the most important go-to tools in your marketing toolkit.

As you can imagine, I spend most of my waking hours thinking, breathing, and living the *Ask Formula*. It's almost become part of my DNA; it's so second nature. But I realize that if you are new to the *Ask Formula*, then it might feel like "drinking out of a fire hose."

That's why I want to recommend that, if possible, you read this section in three ways:

1. **Skim it**. If this is your first time going through this, start at the beginning and give it a quick read all the way through to the end. Don't get bogged down reading it like you were reading a manual. Read it really fast and look at the examples without thinking about your business and how it would work of you. Get a sense of the overall concepts and sequencing of the various parts.

2. **Reread with your business in mind**. When you go back and read it the second time, begin to think about how you might use it for your business. This time when you read

the examples, start to substitute your business and begin to formulate how it might work for you.

3. **Use it as a reference.** Whether through a sophisticated computer program or on the back of a napkin, begin to draft out your own sales funnel using the *Ask Formula*, and sketch out what it might look like. Refer back to this book as you begin implementing the formula in your business. Start the process of asking your market the right questions, and watch the results unfold.

When you are reading for the first time, know that more is coming! If there's something you don't quite "get" at first, keep reading because the more detailed explanation is likely coming up in the next chapter or two. As the concepts become more familiar, you'll begin to see how all the puzzle pieces fit snugly together and form a cohesive element in the overall plan.

You'll also find a Glossary of Terms you can refer to toward the end of the book. This easy reference may help to explain some of the unique language that's used if anything comes up with which you're not familiar.

BIG BENEFIT: DYNAMIC, NOT STATIC

One of the most exciting elements of the *Ask Formula* is that, although it is a formula (meaning that it is a repeatable process with predictable outcomes), the application of that process is dynamic, not static. That is to say, it is always growing, changing, and morphing in *real time*. We are able to refine, optimize, and fine-tune to make it better and more effective with each new application and what we discover in the implementation.

BONUS MATERIAL

That's why I have created an online website that will include special "Bonus" material—which will continue to be updated as technology and market dynamics evolve—and which will give more detail than I'm able to include here, simply because of space limitations. Just please do me a favor, and don't share the following link. I want this to be for verified readers only. (To streamline the text, in places where you might find helpful bonus resources which go deeper on a specific topic, I'll just include the link *http://www.AskFormula.com/bonuses* periodically. When you see that link, you will know there is much more online.)

For example, coming up with the best copy for your emails is an important component to the *Ask Formula*. But this is not a copywriting book. However, you'll find in the bonus site, resources offering guidance to make your emails more powerful and impactful.

Additionally, along with the extra material and information, there is a fast-growing paid community of people who are interested in, and who are implementing the *Ask Formula* in their business. This is a place where I pop in regularly, and where you can ask questions, get clarification, and connect with other savvy business owners who are taking their business to the next level by incorporating the *Ask Formula* into their marketing. If this is something you'd like to be part of, you'll discover how you can become part of this group in the *Next Steps* chapter in this book.

WORD OF CAUTION

The *Ask Formula* has been proven to generate *exceptional* results. Which begs the question: Can this methodology be misused? Of course, most everything can be misused. And if you have the intent of misusing the formula you're about to discover in order to *manipulate* or *mislead*, then please do me a favor and close this book now. This is not for you.

What you're about to discover is powerful. With great power comes great responsibility. The *Ask Formula* is meant to empower people and businesses to more precisely determine what is in the best interest of both the customer and the seller. Use what you're about to discover with *integrity*. Use it for good not evil.

If you and I are on the same page about *doing the right thing*, then without further delay, let's "dive in."

CHAPTER TWELVE

The Process
Prepare, Persuade, Segment, Prescribe, Profit, Pivot

Now that we've covered the story of how the *Ask Formula* was developed, it's time to cover what you probably were hoping to get from this book: the entire formula itself, explained in step-by-step detail.

My goal in this second half of the book is to give you enough detail and guidance so you can apply this for yourself in your own business.

To kick things off, there are two major concepts we need to introduce and differentiate. The first is the *Ask Formula* itself. The second is my *Survey Funnel Strategy*. The best way to think of these two elements is like this:

If the *Ask Formula* is the overriding conceptual framework, then the *Survey Funnel Strategy* is the step-by-step, nuts-and-bolts blueprint to apply that formula in your business online.

The reason it's called the *Survey Funnel Strategy* is because it's a strategy that uses a combination of four specific surveys at four very specific points in your online sales funnel.

If you're not familiar with the term "Sales Funnel"—for our purposes, a Sales Funnel is simply the series of steps you want people to take to go from being a potential customer to becoming an actual customer in your online business.

Many businesses today are using an online sales funnel where a prospect clicks on an online ad, which leads to a landing page (where they're *immediately* asked to enter their name and email address) in exchange for a free report or coupon. Then the prospect is rushed to a "one-size-fits-all" sales copy webpage, followed by a checkout page to enter their payment information. When the sale is made, they send a "thank you" confirming the order. End of story.

The *Survey Funnel Strategy* you're about to discover operates differently—and much, much more effectively.

The pillars of the system are four primary surveys:

1. The "Deep Dive" Survey
2. The "Micro-Commitment Bucket" Survey
3. The "Do You Hate Me" Survey
4. The "Pivot" Survey

These four surveys—and the four big questions they represent—are foundational to the *Ask Formula* because they are the key to finding out exactly what your customers want to buy. If you don't know what the customer wants (or you assume you know what they want), there might be a mismatch between how you're positioning your product and what the market really wants. Even worse, you might be offering the wrong products or services altogether—both of which ultimately lead to losing sales.

To give you an overview of the process, here is a basic "30,000-foot" perspective on the four main surveys in the *Survey Funnel Strategy*.

■ ■ ■

1. THE *DEEP DIVE SURVEY*

This is the foundational survey on which everything else depends. Without this survey all the others fail. This survey collects open-ended data that you'll use to better understand your market in a *deep* way, along with the natural consumer language your market uses. (The exciting news: you can conduct this survey whether you have a list of existing customers or not.)

This opened-ended survey is a survey you conduct once, before you build out your online sales funnel.

So how does this work? If you have a list of customers (or prospective customers) whom you can reach by email, you simply run an open-ended survey sent by email, ask them what their single greatest challenge is (along with several additional questions), and use this information to really figure out who your customer is on a deep (and often more honest) level.

If you don't have a list to mail, you can begin to create a list while at the same time finding out what those customers want to buy by creating a specifically designed landing page to acquire the customer and information. You can also fast-track this process by partnering with someone who *does* have a list—by negotiating a deal that will allow you to send your survey to that person's email list.

If you don't have a list, and you choose to build a landing page and supporting website to acquire survey data—the primary goal of this page or website is not to make money or maximize profit, but to maximize *learning*. This is the substitute for sending an email out to a pre-existing list, and this is how you accomplish that. Based on the results, you'll get information to identify your biggest categories or "buckets" of customers, as well as learn the natural consumer language to use when communicating to each of those customer groups in your marketing. There are some important nuances to this process to ensure you're focusing in on the right data and ignoring the noise in your market, so we'll cover this process in detail in the coming chapters.

Tools: for the *Deep Dive Survey* you can either use an online survey tool like SurveyGizmo (*http://www.AskFormula.com/surveygizmo*) or a tool like Google Forms.

• • •

2. THE *MICRO-COMMITMENT BUCKET SURVEY*

After you've done your homework using the Deep Dive Survey, the results are used to design your "*Micro-Commitment Bucket Survey*," which becomes a permanent part of your online sales funnel. This survey is called what it is because:

a) You're using it to ask people a series of small, *non-threatening*, multiple-choice questions prior to asking more pointed and private questions like "What's your name and email?"— hence, the "Micro-Commitment" part.

b) You're using the answers to those questions to put people into different "buckets" so you can customize your marketing, sales messaging, and the products you introduce to each customer based on what "bucket" (or group) they fall into—hence, the "Bucket" part.

Why put people through a simple survey before asking people for their name and email? The reason is simple: People are generally hesitant to give out their name and email when visiting a new website, and that's understandable. When you start by asking a few simple multiple-choice questions that are far less threatening and personal, it builds "action-taking momentum" toward that final step of entering their name and email.

Secondly, the answers to the multiple-choice questions are data you will capture when your prospects provide their name and email, and opt in to your email list. You'll be able to later use this information to not only customize your marketing messaging, but to also customize the offers you might introduce to that prospect. This is a win-win both for you and the prospective customer.

For example, if you're in a health market, simply knowing whether someone is a man or a woman can help you introduce more targeted offers to each segment. And when you combine that with age information, which you might also capture, you can really get specific.

For instance, if you're in a health-related industry, you might want to introduce a "low testosterone" solution to men in their forties and fifties and perhaps a "menopause" related solution to women in their forties and fifties. If you were to expose your *entire* database to these offers, you might alienate a portion of your audience, and prospective customers would likely unsubscribe from your email list in high numbers over time. But by being able to hyper-target, you ensure that only prospects who are a good potential fit are exposed to your offers.

As you'll discover in the coming chapters, this is just one of the many win-win benefits for both you and your customer for asking for and acquiring this survey data.

When using the most basic application of this survey, oftentimes the question immediately preceding the email opt-in form is what I call the "segmentation question"—a single question that determines which "bucket" that particular prospect will be added to.

Warning: there is a temptation to skip the open-ended *Deep Dive Survey*, and jump right into creating your *Micro-Commitment Bucket Survey*. This is one of, if not *the*, biggest mistakes I see people make when implementing the *Survey Funnel Strategy* in their business. The reason? When we're deeply involved in our market, we think we know what problems our customers run into—and subsequently, what buckets are most worth focusing on.

One of the biggest reasons why the *Ask Formula* has been so successful in the 23 different markets in which I've personally implemented it has been because of the *process*. Whenever my team and I enter a new market, we try to adopt a naïve, beginner's mind—and let the data drive what to do, rather than rush to judgment. The results of your *Deep Dive Survey* will tell you what "buckets" to focus on, and therefore what multiple-choice options to present in your "segmentation question."

In the coming chapters, we'll cover what questions to ask, how to phrase those questions, and how to position your *Micro-Commitment Bucket Survey* so prospective customers are highly motivated to answer your questions.

Tools: for the *Micro-Commitment Bucket Survey*, you can use the same we use in our own implementations and for private clients at *http://www.SurveyFunnelSoftware.com*, or you can use another third-party solution. Alternatively, you can have your own solution coded by a developer on your team or a contractor through a site like oDesk.com or Elance.com.

• • •

3. The "Do You Hate Me?" Survey

This sounds a bit radical, and it is! This is a survey you send by email to everyone who has entered into your email follow-up system, but who has not bought from you after you've presented people with the absolute best deal, price, or promotion you can offer. This survey goes out non-buyers by email to figure out *why* they haven't bought from you.

The strong title of this survey, which gets its name from the email subject I often use when emailing this survey, is designed to get people's attention. However, with such a strong title, you should always make the content of this email lighthearted and even a bit funny. It should ask something like, "What's the single biggest reason why you've decided not to work with me or purchase the XYZ product? Was it something I said? Something I didn't say?" Or "Do you just hate me? :-) Click on this link to let me know."

People are usually so open and forthcoming in responding to this survey. They tell you what hot buttons and objections you haven't done a good job of addressing in your sales messaging. They tell you what you've missed. They give you concrete data to tweak, iterate, and fine-tune your sales funnel over time. It's exceptionally valuable.

Let me use one of my own companies as another example and how I was surprised at what I learned.

I have a paid online mastermind group called the Next Level Group Mastermind. It's a membership community for business owners, many of whom have implemented very successful *Survey Funnels*. The group (I'm honored to say) includes some of the biggest names and leaders in online direct-response marketing. It's a great place to share and get feedback from top marketers around the world specifically for *Survey Funnels*, but for virtually all aspects of an online business as well.

Members of the group can ask questions like: "What do you think about the results of my survey? What changes would you make to the copy on my landing page? How do I get this or that done?"

As part of this mastermind group, members also get access to a monthly mastermind call with me personally, as well as weekly calls with experts I bring in to teach advanced marketing topics.

The members reported they found the group extremely useful and helpful.

That's why I was puzzled and wondered why I wasn't getting more people to join this group. So I decided to run one of my "Do You Hate Me?" surveys to my existing customer list, targeting those who were not members. I asked them honestly, "Why haven't you joined my mastermind group yet?"

The feedback I got was enlightening. People said things like, "Ryan, we actually didn't know you included a monthly mastermind call where you speak to the group personally," and "We didn't know you do live 'hot-seat' style case studies." "We also didn't realize that you bring in marketing experts every single week to talk to the group."

Through this simple email survey, I learned that people weren't joining my membership site because they just didn't have enough information that might have helped them make a decision to join. They were missing some very important pieces of the puzzle. Even though I thought I was doing a great job communicating, I obviously wasn't communicating all the benefits they receive as a member. Needless to say, I was pretty surprised. It wasn't what I expected.

I forwarded this feedback to my team, and told them we need to make the benefits of the mastermind group more prominent in our sales letter. I also followed up to my email list with an FAQ email detailing what we offered in the mastermind group. Bingo. We received a flood of new members. Once again, it proved to me that this kind of surveying, simply asking, gives you the ability to dial in your marketing.

Tools: for the *"Do You Hate Me?" Survey*, you can either use a tool like SurveyGizmo, the *Survey Funnel Software*™ we use, or a simple Google Form.

• • •

4. THE PIVOT SURVEY
This is the final survey in the sequence, also sent out by email. This survey is used after you've done your best job selling your product and the customer simply isn't buying anything you're selling, even after all the surveys, all the emails, and all the dialed-in marketing.

But all is not lost. In this email-survey you say something like, "Hey, listen, I know you're not really interested in what we've been talking about, so which of the following options would you like me to talk about next? Would you like to know about Topic A, or perhaps Topic B, or maybe even Topic C?"

What you're really asking is "What do you want me to try to *sell* you next? You didn't buy this program, but what might you be interested in instead?" This survey is a fantastic tool to employ when you have changed the offer, sent email after email, and just can't get any movement from your prospect. Usually, if your prospect responds to your *Pivot Survey* email, they eventually will buy and you will, without a doubt, increase your conversions.

The *Pivot Survey* is usually a series of links embedded directly into an email. Typically, you'll use your email follow-up system—either through automation links or by setting up different email opt-in forms—to move or add people to different email lists, depending on which option they express interest in. We'll cover this in more detail in the coming chapters.

At a very high level, these are the four pillars of the *Ask Formula* put into practice. The devil is in the details, of course, as well as all the pieces that fit in *between* each of the four surveys. But these four surveys collectively form the foundation, because together, they take all the guesswork out of your marketing. And that is the whole point. How do you succeed in market after market with nearly 100% success? You take out all the guesswork.

Now, we're going to cover the entire *Survey Funnel Strategy* in step-by-step detail—so you can take all the guesswork out of *your* marketing, *and* all the guesswork out of implementing this *process* in your business. As we cover each element in step-by-step detail, feel free to refer to the *Ask Formula* flowchart which graphically illustrates how the process works.

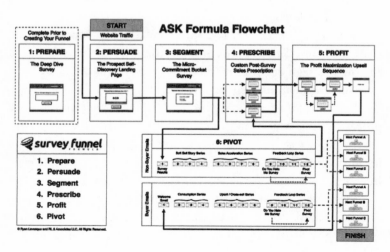

CHAPTER THIRTEEN

Prepare
The Deep Dive Survey

OVERVIEW: THE DEEP DIVE SURVEY

The secret behind creating a super successful *Survey Funnel* starts behind the scenes. It's all about doing your homework and finding out everything you can before you create the rest of your *Survey Funnel*. I'm going to be spending the bulk of this chapter going through what I describe as the "pre-funnel" work—steps you'll be taking *before* you build out your actual sales funnel.

The single most important aspect of the pre-funnel work is your *Deep Dive Survey*. This is something I always carry out before building any sales funnel—and something I can't recommend strongly enough. Before you enter any new market, before you take on any new project, or before you work in any new niche, you must do the *Deep Dive Survey*.

The *Deep Dive Survey* lays the foundation for the rest of the elements in the *Survey Funnel*—everything from your sales copy, to how you segment your market, to how you communicate with each sub-segment differently.

Because of this, it is by far *the most important step* in the entire process. This is why I want to explain exactly what the *Deep Dive Survey* process is, how to implement it, and how you can use the insights you gain from it to set yourself up for success—not only in your *Survey Funnel*, but across your entire business.

Once you know the fundamentals, you can apply this to different broad scenarios that tend to come up *over* and *over again*. I'm going to walk through my exact process for carrying out the *Deep Dive Survey* so you can see how I approach building a funnel

74

and so you can borrow and follow as much of my process as you would like.

> **NOTE about this survey process:** There is a distinct difference between the type of survey work and analysis we will be doing here, and the level of rigor you might expect from a double-blind, placebo-controlled academic medical research study. In other words, there's an "academic" standard of test design and statistical certainty, and a "pracademic" standard. We will be focusing on the latter. The speed of business moves at such a fast pace that "academic" standards are often not feasible—or even prudent—for most small businesses. When it comes to gathering market data, because markets move so quickly, and the opportunity cost of doing nothing while the data rolls in is so high—waiting for statistically valid sample sizes and results with p values < 0.001 is not what we're trying to do here. In other words, everything we do is about being directionally correct rather than achieving absolute statistical certainty.

With that said, let's begin...

■ ■ ■

SO... YOU THINK YOU KNOW YOUR MARKET?

When it comes to the survey process in general, many people love the idea that if they funnel people through a survey they can figure out who their customers are, what they want, and with that information send them to the right pages on their website.

Those pages can be different products you sell, different services you offer or the same product, positioned three, four, or five different ways, based on the answers someone provides to a survey. Now, theoretically, that's great.

But one of the *biggest mistakes* people make going into this process is that they assume they know everything about their prospective customers already and what categories or "buckets" are worth focusing on, especially if it's a market they've been in for a very long time. I see this with the clients I work with all the time—they tell me, "Oh we know our clients. We know who our customers are."

But that is not necessarily true. Many times companies *think* they know, but they really don't. And it costs them big-time in lost sales and revenue.

For example, in one of the sports instructional markets I'm involved in, we discovered through the *Deep Dive Survey* that our hyper-responsive customers (the very most responsive) were 9.4 years older than we thought. On average, they were 64 years old, instead of 55 years old, which this client had been assuming virtually since the inception of their founding.

And by the way, this is an eight-figure business, which was already quite successful. But we used this information to take their sales and profits to the next level. And we did that in part, by fine-tuning their marketing.

For example, this helped us to know who our avatar (representational figure) was—for our online banner advertising. We chose aspirational images of men and women in their mid-sixties instead of their mid-fifties. This had a profound impact.

We fine-tuned our demographic, targeting on Google AdWords and Facebook ads to specifically target the 64-year-old ideal customer. Again, there were huge upticks in the profitability of our advertising.

Then in our emails, we referred to music, movies, and car models that came out when the 64-year-olds were in high school—the most impressionable years of their life. The Rolling Stones playing in a Ford Mustang was more like it! We created feelings of nostalgia that completely missed the mark when our references spanned the wrong decade.

Case in point: When we got our nostalgic references *just right* in the sports instruction market I mentioned above, our email-open rates and click-through rates soared, and sales from our email messages skyrocketed.

And this just scratches the surface.

But this type of deep insight into your market all starts with the *Deep Dive Survey*.

The question is: How do you find out what your customers *really* want—who they are, and how to market to them? How do you put them into "buckets" so you can customize your marketing to them and generate more sales?

The way you figure out what the buckets are, what categories your customers fall into, is to ask a certain set of questions to your audience. It's that simple. *Ask.*

Now, most established companies have a list of existing customers they can survey. Some will not. We'll explore what to do in both situations.

■ ■ ■

If You Have An Existing List

When you have an existing email subscriber list, here are the three basic steps to follow (extensive details to follow):

- **STEP 1: Write an email** that goes out to your list that directs people to take your Deep Dive Survey (which will have a variety of questions in it, including at least one open-ended question).
- **STEP 2: Set up the survey** in a tool like SurveyGizmo or using Google Forms. Capture the data and download the data.
- **STEP 3: Do the analysis** to determine what "bucket" each response falls into, what the sub-buckets are, and what percentage of your market is made up of the various demographic elements that are of interest to you. (The demographics that are of interest to you will vary from market to market—it might be gender, it might be age, but it's important to understand the demographic context of the open-ended survey responses you receive.)
- Identify the *hyper-responsive* customers in your market by using the response-length formula, force multipliers, and scoring system.
- Identify the buckets of hyper-responsive customers, and focus *all* your marketing efforts toward the hyper-responsive segment of your market.

. . .

How is the Analysis Done?

When you do a *Deep Dive Survey* and get all this open-ended question data back, someone has to physically, by hand, look at the information and creatively come up with categories that those fit into.

This is a task to assign to a smart human! People often complain about this part but it cannot be outsourced to a computer.

You do not put the open-ended responses to some machine. Although a machine can analyze word patterns, it can't really tell you what the "buckets" are. You (or someone you assign) will have to look through the responses and give it conscience thought using the process we are going to go through together.

The analogy is like standing in the middle of Times Square. The biggest benefits of going through the *Deep Dive Survey* data yourself is letting it wash over you in the same way if you stand in the middle of Times Square. You might not identify individual faces, but you let the mass of people wash over you, you walk away with a series of lasting, and powerful impressions.

You get the general impression and get the feel of general groups that are present. That immersion process leads to having the deep level of understanding about your market, which your competition will not have. All they have is the surface level.

One level deeper is where you are looking at each individual response for what we define as *hyper-responsiveness*.

These are the responses and respondents which will most likely translate to *customers*. That's why we want to take a look at those responses in detail and think about what close-ended categories those responses might fall into. That requires an intelligent human to go through that process.

That said, finding the right person to review and categorize that data can be outsourced. Analyzing the data is something my team and I do all day every day. That's the reason we often handle the entire process because it does requires a human being who can look at the information and make judgment calls, and this is not something you can outsource to a machine.

The reason why it's so important to ask the open-ended questions is that you can't assume to know more about the prospect than you really do. Most businesses make this critical mistake. This is evident by the fact that most the marketers try to jam their "one-size-fits-all" solution down your throat irrespective of whether or not it is a good fit.

But this isn't the way we operate in person or offline. What is more typical is we ask a series of questions to find out a little about somebody before we presume (or assume) that what we have is right for them.

...

EXAMPLE

The best and easiest real-life example for me to explain how all this works is from my own Marketing Agency and Training business. As we go along, I'll take you through each and every step I have used to implement the *Survey Funnel Strategy*.

To begin, the goal of this particular *Deep Dive Survey* for my Marketing Agency was to learn a few key pieces of information about our prospective customers, so we could eventually direct each visitor to the best-match program or service we offer, based on their particular goals and situation.

STEP 1: WRITING THE EMAIL

The best way to understand what this email should look like—and the entire *Deep Dive Survey* process—is to see an example; below is an email I've sent to my list of email subscribers who have signed up for my free marketing tips at *http://www.FunnelSpecialists.com*. I've sent this email (and ones like it for other businesses) in the past to solicit an audience to take the *Deep Dive Survey*.

The email reads as follows: *"Hey, over the next coming weeks I'd like to do something a little bit different. I thought it would be fun to ask people what they wanted to learn about."*

I then go on to say: *"If you could take just 5 minutes and tell me what is the single biggest challenge that you're struggling with in your business right now... If you could take 30 seconds to tell me what that is, a) it would mean the world to me and b), most importantly, I'll be able to use that information to gear my upcoming emails toward topics you specifically want to know more about."*

Now, the reason why we specifically want to ask about their *single biggest challenge*—and do not overtly and directly ask "What do you want me to sell you?"—goes back to what we talked about earlier when we covered the two types of questions people can accurately answer:

1. What they *don't* want; and
2. Questions about their past behavior.

Asking people what their single biggest challenge is covers *both* of those items. By asking what their single biggest challenge is, you're implicitly asking what challenge *they don't* want to face any more. At the same time, you're implicitly asking about something they've run into in the recent past. It covers both of our bases—without burdening the survey-taker with unnecessary additional questions. (Remember, this is an *open-ended* question we're asking—not a multiple-choice question with a pre-determined set of options.)

If we asked people directly what they want, it forces them to *speculate*—and consider something that may or may not be true. Our minds have a tendency to "invent" things to fill in the gap. In other words, what people *say* they want, what they *think* they want, and what they *really* want (and thus will most likely buy or consume) are different things altogether.

The most accurate representation of what people *really* want comes from identifying what they *don't* want and determining what actions they've taken in the past. Our *Deep Dive Survey* is designed to ferret that information out. And the best part is that this process ultimately benefits both *you* and *your customer*.

INCENTIVES AND DISCOUNTS

By the way, when you run this survey, *do not* offer any sort of costly incentive beyond the result they are looking to get. In other words, no iPad, no free cruise, no Amazon gift card. You do *not* want to offer anything like that.

The only incentive you want to offer is the promise of a solution to their problem. If you include a free gift for taking the survey, your data will be *biased toward people who just want that free thing*. Your data are not going to be representative of whether or not they are a hyper-responsive prospect, and that's what we're looking for here.

If you *do* want to offer some additional incentive to increase your survey uptake rate, that incentive should be a discount off the paid solution to their problem in exchange for their feedback. For example, "As a way of saying thanks for your feedback, you'll receive a 40% discount off the XYZ product/service/program as soon as it becomes available."

The reason this fits our model is because, for someone who has zero or little interest in the solution, offering a discount off of that solution is going to be of zero value to them. So it's not going to sway them to take the survey. Conversely, for someone who is interested in your solution, the discount may be enough to put them over the fence and respond.

You can also couple the discount with a time-sensitive condition to accelerate the pace of survey responses. For example, you can make the discount available to the first X number of respondents, or only until a certain date. Or instead of offering a discount, you can give survey-takers the promise of getting access to the opportunity to buy the solution before it's made available to the general public. However, whatever incentive you offer, it should always be tied to the promise of the solution you're providing. This is an important point.

STEP 2: SETTING UP THE SURVEY

The *Deep Dive Survey* is something you'll direct people to in the email you send out with a link, which directs them to an open-ended survey with the ***Single Most Important Question***

(Note: Bonus Material available at: *http://www.AskFormula.com/bonuses.*)

(i.e. the first question you ask in your *Deep Dive Survey*, which represents the single most important piece of information you want to gather. In this case, that piece of information is identifying the survey-taker's "single biggest marketing challenge.") The webpage looks like this image on pg. 81.

UGLY BUT EFFECTIVE

Now, if you're like most people, your first reaction might be: This survey is kind of "ugly," what gives? The survey is actually "ugly" on purpose. In fact, generally speaking, you actually want to turn away people who will be turned off by an ugly presentation.

Why? It's like this: If you were to receive a phone call from a number that looks to be a telemarketer, in which the caller's voice is all garbled and the connection is terrible, you're probably going to hang up on that person, right? But, if you've been waiting all day for some important medical results from your doctor and recognize the number on your phone, but *his/her* voice is all garbled and the connection is terrible—you're probably going to stay on the phone until you can make out what is being said.

In both cases, the voice quality (the "presentation") is identically "ugly." But in the second case, you *care enough* about the information to stick around *in spite* of that ugly presentation. By making your survey *ugly*, you actually create a response bias in favor of people who care enough about the topic to respond in spite of that ugly presentation.

Let's look at the question on that screen, *"What's your #1 single biggest marketing challenge you're struggling with right now?"* This is the single most important question you can ask in the *Deep Dive Survey*, which is why I almost always recommend *starting* with this open-ended question. The reason why is because if someone starts to fill out your survey but doesn't answer *all* the questions, at a bare minimum you want them to *at least* answer this one question.

TITLES FOR SORTING

More than likely, you'll be running multiple surveys to multiple segments of your list, so you'll want to easily separate the data based on the source from where the survey-takers are coming.

Typically, I use a three-letter code, SFF, which stands for the particular project, *Survey Funnel Formula*, and a four-letter code that stands for the list from where people came. In the case of our example, "SFF-FNSP" is a template. (This isn't an actual survey I use but it's the template built for all the surveys I ran to the various segments of our FunnelSpecialists.com email list [FNSP for Funnel Specialists] to get this data.)

For example, I like to separate the data from buyers of different products. So we send these groups of people copies of the same survey, to keep the data separate within the survey tool we're using.

In our real data, examples would include GLPC, which stands for *Green Light Project Checklist* customers who purchased our *Green Light Project Checklist* course—*http://www.GreenLight-ProjectChecklist.com* (a training program on how to choose and evaluate new markets to enter, projects to launch, and products to sell)—and GLPP, which stands for *Green Light Project Checklist* prospects (people who signed up to learn more about that product, but who ultimately did not purchase).

If you sell multiple products or product types—or if you have multiple channels where people might sign up for your email list—it's important to have a coding system in your survey so you know where your prospects and customers are coming from to give you a little bit of context behind the answers they give you.

In our example, if you were to answer that first open-ended question and click *Next* in our example, this is the question you'll see on the next screen:

The reason why I've asked this question next after our open-ended "Single Most Important Question" is because, of the remaining questions I want to ask, this is the lowest-threshold question (by that I mean a question that is most non-threatening).

The reasons it's "non-threatening" is because it only requires an "A" or "B" response. It does not require much thought to answer. There's a clear line in the sand (you're either A or B, with little room for ambiguity) and it doesn't require revealing any type of sensitive information.

What I'm also doing here is "testing" a question I might consider including in my *Micro-Commitment Bucket Survey* (which I'll explain in more detail) as part of my ongoing, new-lead-acquisition process. I want to see what this A/B percentage breakdown looks like among my current subscriber base.

The low-threshold question you might ask here will vary based on the market you're in.

In many of the markets I'm in—including virtually all the health, fitness, and sports instruction markets—this low-threshold, A/B question is often "Are you a man or a woman?" You might consider doing the same thing, if gender provides useful context or is relevant to the information and marketing message you might deliver.

In this case, gender didn't really matter, so I started with a single A/B question that is relevant. I really wanted to know if people are full-time entrepreneurs—whether their Internet business is their full-time income or if they have a separate day job.

If you select "My Internet business is my full-time income," and click the *Next* button you will see the question: *Which of the following best describes you?*

SFF-FNSP: Tell me a little about your situation... (from Ryan Levesque)
New Page

3. **Which of the following best describes you?**

○ I'm a biz owner. Mostly sell my OWN products.
○ I'm a biz owner. Mostly sell AFFILIATE products.
○ I'm a copywriter.
○ I'm a marketing consultant who helps biz owners.
○ I'm an employee of a company.
○ Something completely different:

Back　Next
33%

The reason for this question is because I'm *fishing* for potential "buckets." To be clear, I am using the initial, open-ended "Single Most Important Question" to tell me what the *actual* buckets are going to be. (I'll explain the process in detail because it's a relatively advanced technique. It's also something almost *nobody* does, which helps set you apart from your competition.) Right now, I'm trying to figure out, based on the "gut feeling" I get from my knowledge of the market, whether the buckets I think exist are actually representative of the market.

What's interesting in *this* example is that it turned out that my "gut feeling" was wrong—and because of that, I want to show you how the actual open-ended results compared to what I *thought* the market to be. You'll see how *even after* you've gone through this process hundreds of times, across dozens of markets, as I have myself, you still want to let the *data* guide your decision-making. To paraphrase: A beginner's mind is a Zen mind.

In this question, you'll notice I also like to include a write-in answer as the final option to see if I'm missing the mark. This is yet another data point to help you figure out the most important buckets worth focusing in on.

> **IMPORTANT NOTE:** with the exception of that last open-ended write-in option, whenever you present multiple-choice options like this, to eliminate biases, ideally, you want to *randomize* the order in which you present those multiple-choice options. The reason why is because people will tend to skew toward selecting the *first* and *last* multiple-choice options they're presented with. If you've studied the science of memory encoding and consolidation, then you'll be familiar with the *primacy* and *recency* effects. In plain English, in a list of items—the first and last item tend to stand out more in our minds than everything in the middle. So it's important to eliminate that bias.

The next question you'll see is: *"Roughly, what's the overall size of your own business in terms of gross sales $?"*

SFF-FNSP: Tell me a little about your situation... (from Ryan Levesque)
New Page

4. Roughly, what's the overall size of your own business in terms of gross sales $?

○ < $100k / year
○ $100k - $499k / year
○ $500k - $999k / year
○ $1M - $1.9M / year
○ $2M - $4.9M / year
○ $5M+ / year

Back Next
50%

The reason I want to know the size of the business is because, in the next steps of the *Survey Funnel* I'm intending to build, this is relevant to what product or service we might recommend for a given business.

In this example, for my agency to create and implement a full sales funnel build-out, a business that's making less than $100,000/year is not going to be a good candidate, because a) they generally don't have the money to invest, and b) even if they did, it just doesn't make sense to pay the fees involved in designing and building a sales funnel, because they may not get an immediate ROI, which they probably need.

A business making less than $100,000/year would be a good candidate for a variety of services provided by my agency. They might even be a fit for one of our coaching or consulting options.

A business doing five million dollars a year or more *would* likely be a very good candidate for a full sales funnel build-out through our agency, because they'll likely see a solid ROI. So, I want to get a sense for what the breakdown of my market looks like.

The point is, we're identifying extremes so we can decide where to best target our efforts.

The next question in the *Deep Dive Survey* in our example is: *"What's your primary niche/market?"*

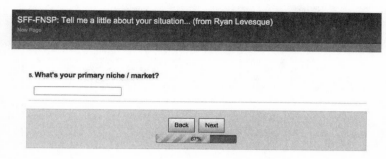

The reason I want to know the answer to *this* question is because, when I'm talking about case studies in my marketing, I want to make those case studies as *relevant* as possible. It's important to know if someone sells industrial equipment as a wholesaler—or if someone publishes instructional information online selling directly to consumers (to cover two potential extremes).

The more you can "dimensionalize" your prospect with questions like these, the better—especially when it comes to sharing case studies, success stories, testimonials, and customer feedback.

The flip side of the coin is this: With every additional question you ask—you will start to see a *drop-off* in response. For example, for every 100 people who answer the first question in your survey, you might only see 60-70% answer the fifth question. These numbers will vary widely depending on a number of different factors, including how passionate your survey-takers are about the subject matter, how deep their relationship is with you, how much they care about finding a solution to their problem, whether you're operating in a business-to-business market or business-to-consumer market, etc.

Generally speaking, you *should expect* to see a degradation in response the deeper you get into your survey. So, for this reason, it's essential to prioritize the importance of your questions beyond the initial questions in your survey.

The other consideration is the fact that, in most cases, you will want *complete* survey responses—which include a survey-taker's name, email, and phone number on the very last step of the survey, which, in our example, looks like this:

The reason why you want this information is because we'll be using it whether or not someone provides their contact information as an important data point when analyzing your survey responses. All things being equal, someone who provides their full contact information and gives you permission to contact them by phone is a *better* prospect (and more likely to be a buyer) than someone who wishes to remain anonymous.

For this reason, you can see here on this last step I've asked:

> *"Lastly, I may want to follow up with a few people personally to learn about your situation. If you'd be open to chatting for a few minutes on the condition that I promise not to sell you anything—please leave your name and phone number below."*

This specific language used here is important: The promise of *not* selling anything is key. Your goal here is to see who is willing to provide their phone number to you, because we'll be using this data as part of our formula for scoring the *quality* of responses.

By the end of this process, you want to become so familiar with your market that you know where they hang out on the weekend, what they smell like, and what they watch on TV on a Friday night. You want to know the book that's on their bedside nightstand, what car they drive; you want to know all these things.

(For this reason, I'll often get on the phone with survey-takers to get an even *deeper* understanding of their situation.)

All of this data gives you a complete, multidimensional view of your prospect, so that when you communicate with them in your marketing—whether that's through video, email, or sales copy on your website—to them, it feels like you almost know them personally. In fact, when you do this right—customers and prospects will write to you and say: *"It's like you know what's going on in my head and you can read my mind."*

And that does *not* happen by chance. It happens because you've developed such a deep, intimate understanding of your market by gathering (and analyzing) the *Deep Dive Survey* data in your market. So now let's talk about how to analyze all the data once you've acquired it.

STEP 3: DO THE ANALYSIS

This is where things start to get interesting. This is where you get to start digging into your data and begin analyzing your market, which will give you everything you need to design your own *Survey Funnel* style sales funnel for your business.

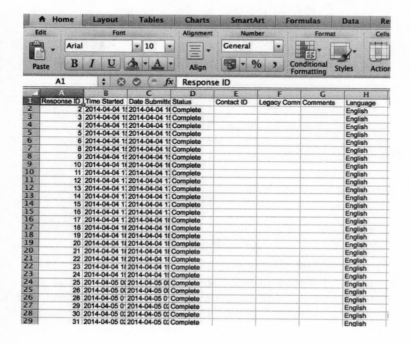

This first step in the process is to download your survey data from whichever survey software you're using into a spreadsheet. If you're using SurveyGizmo, then your raw data will look something like the image on page 89.

Most of the data we don't really care about. Things like Session ID, User Agent, and IP Address are *not* data points we'll be using in our analysis, so you'll want to hide those columns from view to focus on the important stuff. What we really care about are the columns with our survey questions responses.

In this next section, you'll discover how to transform this raw data into something that's actually useful to understand your market in a very deep way and then which data you'll use to help design your online sales funnel.

Here is what the data looks like from our example, after I've organized it in a Microsoft Excel spreadsheet:

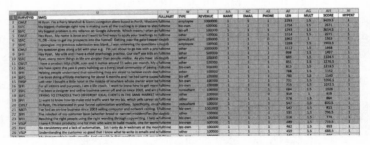

(Note: Bonus Material available at: *http://www.AskFormula.com/bonuses.*)

Let's go through each column in this spreadsheet, so you can understand what we're looking at and how to organize your data in the same way.

COLUMN A: SURVEYID

The first thing I like to do is add a column on the far left, called SURVEYID. This column simply helps you identify where the data came from if you're running copies of the survey to multiple segments of your list.

For example, as you can see from my SurveyGizmo dashboard, I ran copies of the same survey to multiple segments of my list. The identifying codes SFF-VSLP, SFF-VSLC, etc. indicate where the responses came from. You'll notice that Column A lists this data point.

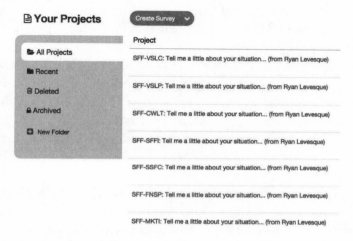

COLUMN U: SMIQ (SINGLE MOST IMPORTANT QUESTION)

Between Column A and Column U, I've "hidden" all the data we won't be using (e.g., Session ID, IP Address) to simplify what we're looking at. Column U is where we list the answers to our open-ended Single Most Important Question (SMIQ).

COLUMNS V, W, X

This is where we list what categories each respondent falls into in each of our multiple-choice questions:

- Column V: Full-Time vs. Part-Time (FULLPART)
- Column W: Biz Owner, Consultant, Employee, etc. (TYPE)
- Column X: Revenue category (REVENUE)

COLUMNS AA, AC, AE

In these columns, we use a simple formula that spits out a 1 if the field in the previous column contains data and is not blank.

For example, if someone provides their PHONE in Column AD (which is hidden), Column AE spits out a 1. If they do NOT provide their PHONE in Column AD, Column AE spits out a 0.

This allows you to sort all the people who provided their name, email, and phone number—which, as you'll see in a moment, we'll be using in our analysis.

Column AF: LEN

In this column, we use an MS Excel formula called "length" (LEN) to calculate the number of characters from our prospect's response to our open-ended SMIQ. This tells us how long each prospect's response is.

The reason why response length is vitally important is because it's an indication of hyper-responsiveness, which is a *leading indicator* of how likely someone is to purchase a paid solution for the problem or challenge about which we're asking.

In plain English, all things being equal, the *longer a prospect's open-ended response is, the more likely they are to be a buyer* of whatever it is you're selling.

For example, let's say you're selling a medical device that helps reduce back pain, and if you, as the business owner, ask, "What's the single biggest challenge you're having with back pain right now?"

Let's pretend someone types in, *"My back hurts."*

And the second person types in, *"Five years ago I got into a car accident; it was a head-on collision; I had to go through physical therapy for six months; I went through three different back-pain medications; I was even on morphine for a period of time; I've been out of work for the last two-and-a-half years; I can't hold down a stable job and it's all because I can't sit down in an office chair and I've been trying to find a solution for the last five years and I'm desperate to find anything that works."*

Which of those two respondents is more likely to purchase a product if you have a solution that solves their problem? The second one, of course. This is why we pay attention to response length, and why it's so important.

Column AG: MULT

The next column is MULT, which stands for **multiplier**. This column uses a simple MS Excel formula to check if the PHONE field is > 0 (i.e., if someone has provided us with their phone number). If they have, then the formula spits out a 1.5. If the person did not provide their phone number, it spits out a 1.0.

The reason this column is called MULT is because we will multiply the output of this formula (either 1.0 or 1.5) to the LEN column (response length) to give us a relative SCORE for each prospect.

The reason why we apply this "force multiplier" of 1.5 to people's responses if they leave their phone number is because when someone leaves their phone number and is willing to talk to you on the phone about the challenge they're facing, they are more likely to be a potential buyer.

In fact, on average, I've found that when someone leaves their phone number—when controlling for response length—that person is roughly 50% more likely to purchase from you than someone who provides a text response of the same length, but who does not provide their phone number.

Naturally, this number will vary from market to market, and business to business. But generally speaking, it's wise to apply more weight to a response that includes a phone number as well—and in the absence of data in your market, 50% is a reasonable place to start.

This brings us to the next column—SCORE.

Column AH: SCORE

After you've gone through this entire process, you will be left with a SCORE for each response. Here you'll notice that the scores are organized in descending order—starting with the highest score at the top and the lowest score at the bottom.

This sets you up for the next and final column at this stage of the process: HYPER.

Column AI: HYPER

Earlier we talked about the importance of focusing 100% of your marketing on your most hyper-responsive prospects and customers, individuals who are *most* likely to purchase from you. The entire *Deep Dive Survey* analysis we've gone through up until this point has been designed to *identify* who those *hyper-responsive* individuals are, based on the score we've attached to each response.

From here forward, we are going to primarily focus on the Top 20% of your market, and to a lesser extent, the 20% below that—according to response SCORE. Anyone in the Top 20% of your market gets a "1" in this column. And if you have fewer than

100 responses in this Top 20%, I generally like to look at the 20% below that to have more data to work with.

X	AA	AC	AE	AF	AG	AH	AI
REVENUE	**NAME**	**EMAIL**	**PHONE**	**LEN**	**MULT**	**SCORE**	**HYPER?**
1000000	1	1	1	2293	1.5	3439.5	1
500000	1	1	1	1754	1.5	2631	1
100000	1	1	1	1743	1.5	2614.5	1
100000	1	1	1	1514	1.5	2271	1
100000	1	1	0	1962	1	1962	1
100000	1	1	1	1269	1.5	1903.5	1
1000000	1	1	1	1112	1.5	1668	1
500000	1	1	1	998	1.5	1497	1
100000	1	1	1	883	1.5	1324.5	1
100000	1	1	1	851	1.5	1276.5	1
500000	1	1	1	813	1.5	1219.5	1
100000	1	1	1	768	1.5	1152	1
100000	1	1	1	760	1.5	1140	1
100000	1	1	1	731	1.5	1096.5	1
100000	1	1	1	715	1.5	1072.5	1
100000	1	1	1	684	1.5	1026	1
100000	1	1	0	919	1	919	1
100000	1	1	1	576	1.5	864	1
100000	1	1	1	547	1.5	820.5	1
1000000	1	1	1	542	1.5	813	1
100000	1	1	1	531	1.5	796.5	1
100000	1	1	1	516	1.5	774	1
500000	1	1	1	489	1.5	733.5	1
100000	1	1	1	462	1.5	693	1

A quick note about the data in this example: Because I'm fortunate to have the experience of going through this process in dozens of markets, I know that the scores we're seeing here are extremely high. Most marketers will not see response scores like we're seeing here, and there are several reasons for that.

First, it has to do with my positioning in the marketplace. In my market, prospective customers really do want to get on the phone with me, personally. Since my phone-consulting rate is several thousand dollars per hour, this survey implies the opportunity to get on the phone with me without paying that rate (in actuality, I do get on the phone periodically and talk to people so this isn't just a tease.)

Second, this is going out to a warm audience. These are people who know me. Typically, they are existing customers who have bought products—and sometime multiple products—from me before.

Third, many prospective customers know me as the *Survey Funnel* guy, so they're going to complete any survey I put out, just to see the process of how I do things.

The reason why I'm telling you this is because it's unlikely you'll see the kind of numbers I'm showing you in your market—especially if you're acquiring data from cold traffic. And if you do not see scores this high, I don't want you to be discouraged. Generally speaking, anything over a score of 400, using the formula I've outlined for you, is a good indicator that you've got a segment of your market that's *hyper-responsive* and worth focusing on.

THE DEMOGRAPHICS

So where do you go from here? Before we get into how to analyze your open-ended responses, I want to show you how to analyze and what to do with the demographic/categorical data we've acquired.

In our example, I was very interested to discover the percentage of people who were full-time versus part-time, what percentage of people were business owners who sell their own product versus affiliate products, and the revenue breakdown of my customers.

80/20 FOCUS (ADDRESSING 80% OF THE MARKET WHILE FOCUSING ON THE TOP 20% OF RESPONSES)

What I'm looking to find out is the *80/20* of each question. In other words, across each of these parameters, where does the majority (roughly 80%) of the market fall? The reason I want to know this is because if I'm only going to focus on one segment of my market, I want to know: How do I get the biggest bang for my buck? What does that *one* segment look like? And then, if I'm going to focus on two segments, what do those *two* segments look like? Etc. etc.

Ideally, I'm trying to reach 80% of my market, with as few "buckets" as possible. (And this is important.) Every additional "bucket" you add creates more work and more complexity. Putting your market into different "buckets" and speaking to each of those buckets differently is extremely powerful. It's the crux to my entire marketing approach. But if you can get away with reaching 80% of your market without having to do any sort of segmentation, then this exercise will tell you that.

Similarly, if you do plan on developing a full-blown *Survey Funnel* style sales funnel, and want to get "version 1.0" of your sales funnel off the ground immediately, this exercise will help you identify the segment worth speaking to directly, if you were forced to choose only *one*.

What I've done here is look at each of
the main parameters in which I'm interested:

full-time	70%
day job	30%
biz-own	45.50%
biz-aff	5.40%
employee	4.50%
consultant	19.80%
copywriter	2.30%
other	22.30%
<$100K	67.60%
$100k-500k	18.90%
$500k-999k	6.30%
$1M-1.9M	4.50%
$2M-4.9M	1.80%
$5M+	0.90%
Phone?	70.50%

FULL-TIME VERSUS DAY JOB
You'll notice, for this question, the market
skews heavily 70/30 toward full-time
business owners.

BUSINESS TYPE
In this example, the market is roughly 65%
business owners who sell their own prod-
uct and consultants. What about the "other" bucket? Given the
relatively high 22% number, this had me concerned I'd missed the
mark with the multiple-choice options. However, after reviewing those responses in detail, interestingly, the majority of people
who selected "other" turned out to be business owners who sell
their own product *and* do consulting as well. Combined with the
open-ended responses in this third "hybrid" category, business
owners who sell their own product (and who do it with or without consulting as part of their business) represents over 65% of
my market.

BUSINESS SIZE
As far as business size, 85% of people have businesses that generate
under $500,000/year in sales, and nearly 68% under $100,000/
year in sales. As I think about how this might correspond to our
product mix, it tells me I can probably steer about 65% of people
into our Training Courses, and another 20% of people into our
Coaching & Mastermind Programs, and then another 15% represent larger businesses that might be candidates for our Agency
Level Sales Funnel Implementation.

This gives me a rough idea of the market we're working with.
It also tells me if we had to choose just *one* segment of the market
to focus on, our customer avatar might look like this:

*Full-time business owner who sells his own product, and is earn-
ing < $100,000 per year in his business.*

NOTE: This is something of a simplification to illustrate this step of the process. When you go through this exercise yourself, you'll also want to look at the interaction between each variable. For example, it's likely that the 70% of full-time business owners skew toward a higher average revenue. I know, for example, from analyzing the data that virtually 100% of the businesses earning at least $100,000/year or more fall within the "full-time" category.

CATEGORIZING THE OPEN-ENDED RESPONSES AND MINING THEM FOR *GOLD*

The next part of the *Deep Dive Survey* analysis is arguably the most important step of the entire process. This is where you'll be looking at the *open-ended* Single Most Important Question, coming up with categories for each response, and compiling the "natural consumer language" your market uses, so you can echo that language back when you communicate with your market.

In other words, you'll be mining these open-ended responses for gold—again, focusing on the Top 20% of responses.

WHAT ARE YOU USING THESE RESPONSES FOR?

- To determine what **buckets** naturally emerge in your market.
- To identify what people's **hot buttons** are.
- To identify what their **objections** are.
- To identify what their biggest **challenges** are.
- To use in concert with their **demographic** information.

Simply put, you're going to use the results of this analysis to figure out what buckets to send people to when building out your *Micro-Commitment Bucket Survey*.

How do these buckets differ from the demographic exercise we just went through? Analyzing the demographics of your market, as we did in the preceding section, will tell you *who your prospective customers are*. Analyzing your open-ended responses will tell you what those customers want to buy.

It's important to know that someone is a full-time business owner, selling their own product, making less than $100,000/year. Now that I know that about our market—I won't talk about the struggle of moonlighting as an entrepreneur while juggling a day job in my marketing.

But what's even more important is understanding the *struggle* that full-time business owner making less than $100,000/year is having right now *specifically*—and thus, what problem they're most likely to be willing to spend money to solve.

The way we do this is by looking at the open-ended responses people provide (focused on the Top 20%, and to a lesser extent the 20% below that, according to our SCORE system). We then categorize those responses into multiple "buckets" to identify trends. After your first pass, it's common to have dozens and dozens of buckets. *Having too many buckets is just as problematic as having no buckets at all.*

So you want to combine and consolidate those buckets until you're left with, ideally, three to five buckets that address 80% of your market. You'll almost never be able to address 100% of your market, because there will generally be outlier responses that are so far afield from the rest of your market, that you would have to develop custom, unique solutions for each of those individuals.

Why three to five buckets? These buckets will correspond to the different segments in your market that you address differently in your sales funnel either through:

- Different messaging.
- Different products you sell.
- A combination of the above.

In my experience, I've found that three to five buckets is generally the "sweet spot" that'll give you 80% of the results that segmentation provides. Theoretically, you can make an argument for 100 different buckets—because, after all, every prospective customer is an individual with unique needs, wants, and desires. But if you're like most people, you can see why this simply isn't practical.

Imagine having 100 possible sales pages on your website to purchase a single product. I've seen what happens when marketing segmentation projects are overly ambitious: *The complexity kills the project before it gets off the ground.*

Three to five buckets is manageable and, when done correctly, provides a *massive* return. If this is your first time going through this process, I urge you to stick to the "three-to-five-buckets" rule. So let's dive into the process of categorizing your open-ended responses and coming up with your buckets.

You'll notice here in our spreadsheet that we've got three columns: CAT 1, CAT 2, and CAT 3.

The reason for this is, for each open-ended response, I like to apply no more than three different categories to that response. Every single response will have at *least* one category—but sometimes people will refer to multiple topics in their responses, and you'll want the flexibility to capture that information in different columns. Three columns is a good starting point to avoid making this part of the process overly complex.

L	M	N
CAT 1	CAT 2	CAT 3
PPC Conversion	SellOther: Non-Info	Offline Sales Process
Tracking	Product Sequencing	Backend Products
PPC Conversion	PPC Compliance	
SellOther: Services		
Offline sales process		
New Business/Market		
Cold traffic conversion		
Multiple Sub-Markets	Many Products	
N/A		
Fix/Improve/Optimize Funnel		
Add Revenue stream: Advertising		
Skeptical prospects		
Technical concerns	New business / market	
Better Survey: Lead strategy		
Better Survey: Lead strategy	More leads	
Technical concerns	What tools	
Multiple Sub-Markets		
Cold traffic conversion	multiple sub markets	
Fix/Improve/Optimize Funnel	what tools	
Fix/Improve/Optimize Funnel	USP	
Sell Want / Give Need		
Multiple Sub-Markets	Market understanding	
Multiple Sub-Markets	Product Sequencing	

To understand the process of how to take a long, open-ended response and break it down into series of closed-ended categories, it's helpful to see an example. In the first row of the data we're working with, the person's open-ended response is the following:

Hi Ryan. I'm a Perry Marshall & Glenn Livingston client based in Perth, Western Australia. Gigging as the marketing manager for URL.com. My biggest challenge is improving our conversion rates. We spend $35K/m on AdWords, and it just keeps getting more expensive over time (avg CPC went up 47% in the last 6 months!) even though I am Perry trained, 8 yrs managing adwords with high QS & so forth. Our leads cost ~$100 each (conv rate ~10%) and about 1 in 10 of them converts to a sale (i.e. cost per sale ~$1000!), and we only make $1500-1600 per sale in gross profit. Avg CPC $10-13 :-(In other words, we are still in the red once we pay for the ads and staff to do everything. Split testing is difficult AND expensive (@ $10+ per click), so it's mega tough running long statistically significant tests, etc. I want to use surveys, autoresponders, etc to help build a list, bond with them and ultimately increase our conversions and ROI, but I am not really having any luck there. Let alone building a full-on high performing funnel like you might be able to. Almost all the training I see for this sort of stuff is targeted at business selling coaching or services, not classic B2B products like car loans, etc. Plus, 99% of people who come to us are just chasing a quote for a loan (i.e. what interest rate do I qualify for, etc.) and don't tend to want us to keep communicating with them. Unlike Lending Tree (in the USA), we can't give confirmed quotes online. We have to speak with the applicant on the phone, collect their info and submit a loan application to 1 or more lenders and see how they rate the client & deal. They then come back to use with a rate and whether or not the client got approved or not. It makes it a lot tougher because people really can't easily price shop us without having to speak with a finance consultant. Obviously that puts a lot of people off, hence the only 10% conv rate from visit to lead. I would LOVE to get some ideas on how to build a quality funnel for my kind of business that increases ROI, etc. PLUS, if there was actually a way you could work with us directly and help significantly improve results, I would be happy to work with you to figure out how in the heck I could sell that idea to the company owners... :-) Thanks in advance.   EM

Essentially, this gentleman runs the marketing for a car-loan lead-generation business online in Australia and is wondering how to make Pay Per Click (PPC) traffic convert in a competitive, high-cost environment.

This response is a good example, because it represents one we could approach in several different ways. That said, the categories I came up with for his response were as follows:

Since he wanted to know how to apply my techniques to PPC, essentially getting PPC traffic to convert, I've called the first category "PPC conversion."

Next, he wanted to know how to apply my techniques to sell non-information products; he talked about a lot of the sales funnel training online talks about selling info products and coaching services and things of that nature but wasn't sure how to apply it to his business. So I've called the second category "SellOther: Non-Info."

After that, he wanted to know how to apply his techniques to an offline sales process, because in his business he's not able to transact directly online. He has to take the process over the phone do to regulatory issues around making quotes for car loans online in Australia. So I've called the third category "Offline Sales Process."

This is essentially the process you'll want to go through for each of your Top 20% responses (and the 20% below that, if you have fewer than 100 Top 20% responses). This represents your first pass through the data.

NARROW DOWN YOUR BUCKETS BY *COMBINING* AND *CONSOLIDATING* CATEGORIES

The first time you go through your data, it's likely you'll have dozens and dozens of different categories. But the name of the game isn't to have an infinite number of buckets. The name of the game is to cover 80% of your market with three to five buckets. So you will likely need to make a few additional passes through the data.

In your first pass, you want to look for categories that are very similar to one another, or even identical, but for which you've applied different labels. For these, you want to use the same naming convention and combine them into a single category.

For example, I had labeled the first category in our example "PPC Conversion" and noticed later on I had labeled another category from another response "Converting PPC Traffic."

For all intents and purposes, these two categories represent the same issue—so I renamed them both "PPC Conversion." That's your first pass.

In your second pass, you want to look for multiple sub-buckets that occur in small volume, which you can potentially combine into one larger bucket.

For example, I noticed there were a large number of people who had very specific technical concerns about building out their own *Survey Funnel,* so I created a category called "Technical Concerns" as a way to combine these responses together into one larger bucket.

At this stage, you'll likely have what will become your "sub-buckets." And now it's a matter of grouping those sub-buckets into different "themes."

For example, several sub-buckets that emerged in my survey included:

- Cold Traffic Conversion
- PPC Conversion
- PPC Compliance
- AdWords Conversion
- Bing Conversion

I consider these all part of the same overall theme. So while preserving these individual sub-bucket names and the number of responses for each, I've grouped them into a larger bucket I call "PPC/Cold Traffic Conversion."

Once you've gone through the process of combining all your sub-buckets into different "themes," you want to sort those themes in descending order, based on the number of individual responses covered by each theme.

Your goal is to get to the point where 80% of your responses are covered by three to five different "themes." These themes represent the "buckets" you'll focus on in customizing your marketing messaging and the products you offer to each segment of your market. By preserving the individual sub-buckets within each theme, you'll be able speak to each individual point when addressing that bucket in your marketing.

For example, I know that when addressing my "PPC/Cold Traffic Conversion" bucket, I need to specifically address PPC advertising, PPC compliance, and more specifically mention Google AdWords, and Yahoo/Microsoft Bing Advertising.

All of these items are part of the same theme, but none of these categories are high-volume enough to warrant being their own bucket. However, it would make sense for me to speak to each of these sub-buckets *directly* within the context of my overall marketing message to the larger bucket as a whole, because these are the most important issues that came up.

When going through this process yourself in your business, *you will be making judgment calls* as to how you group your sub-buckets and organize your buckets. This is perfectly normal. (In fact, learning how to make judgment calls is one of the many benefits of the Next Level Group Mastermind, *http://www.NextLevelGroup-Mastermind.com*, the paid online community of business owners who are implementing *Survey Funnels*, because it can be helpful to get perspective from other marketers who have gone through this process when you're not sure how to segment your market.)

Now that we've covered the *Deep Dive Survey* foundational pre-funnel work, let's talk about what to do if you do NOT have an existing email list of customers or prospects to run your *Deep Dive Survey*.

■ ■ ■

IF YOU DO *NOT* HAVE AN EXISTING LIST

The question I know some people might have is, *"What if I don't have an email list? How do I do this?"* This is something I can completely relate to, because I was in this exact situation when we decided to enter the memory-improvement market. If you don't already have an existing email list, you have two main options:

1. You can use someone else's email list to run your *Deep Dive Survey*—either by asking a friend or paying to "rent" another business's email list. (Note: Bonus Material available at: *http://www.AskFormula.com/bonuses.*) The major benefit to this option is that it's faster and often less expensive than option # 2. The major downside is that, unless you plan on *selling* to the email list you rent or borrow to run your *Deep Dive Survey*, that list of subscribers—and the way they respond to your survey—might not be indicative of the overall market as a whole.

2. You can drive cold paid traffic to a "landing page" on your website, requesting people to complete your *Deep Dive Survey*. The major benefit to this option is that it gives a good, true indication of what the market *as a whole* is struggling with—and this is especially useful if you plan on sending paid traffic to your future sales funnel (because you'll be gathering *Deep Dive Survey* data on that same audience). The major downside is that it will generally take longer and cost a bit more than the first option.

Creating a Landing Page

If you go with the second option, and you don't have a website for the new market or business you're considering pursuing, then you'll need to create one. If that's the case, here's the process you'll need to follow in a nutshell:

- Set up a simple site with a Landing Page and a two-step email opt-in process, whereby you simultaneously obtain a prospect's name and email address (to build your email list) as well as the answer to your *Single Most Important Question* from your *Deep Dive Survey* (to accumulate survey data).

- Your Landing Page should not have a form on the page itself. Instead, that page should have a mix of text and graphics explaining what you're offering in exchange for the prospect's feedback, followed by a link, button, or combination thereof which directs people to the second page in the sequence, which contains a form with your survey question or questions. (See below for an example of the *form page*.)

- Since this is cold traffic, the incentive for filling out the form should be some sort of "ethical bribe," like a free report or kit that's positioned to solve the single biggest challenge you're asking prospects to tell you about in your survey.
- Once you accumulate enough survey responses, you'll want to analyze the data in the same way we just covered.

Let's take a look at an example. Here's the actual *Deep Dive Survey form page* we created when entering the memory-improvement instructional market. Prior to building our RocketMemory™ website, we built a temporary site (which is no longer active today) called Total Memory Improvement, with the objective of gathering market research.

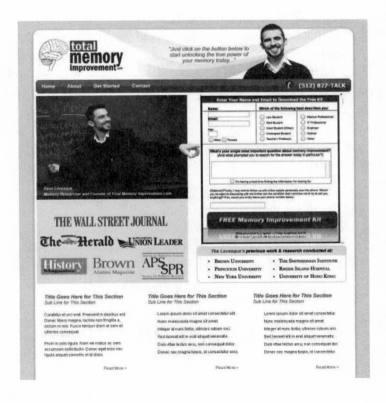

On this page, we offered prospects a "Free Memory Improvement Kit" in exchange for telling us a little about their situation (the ethical bribe). As you can see, the form asked for name, email, and some demographic information (including age, gender, and their professional situation).

Here's the important part: You'll also notice I asked our *Deep Dive Survey* open-ended question: *"What's your single most-important question about memory improvement? And what prompted you to search for the answer today in particular?"*

Here's where things differ from the *Deep Dive Survey* that might be sent to an existing email list: In the case of this example, I was sending traffic from Google AdWords and the Yahoo/ Bing Network—advertising with keywords such as "Improve Memory" and "How to Improve Memory." In other words, when someone searched for the term "How to Improve Memory," my ads would show up on the first page of Google. If they clicked on my ad, they were directed to the Landing Page you see above.

Now, the reason for asking *both* open-ended questions (unlike in the *Deep Dive Survey* you might send to an existing email list) is because you want to know not *only* what their single biggest question or challenge is; you also want to know *why* they decided to search for a solution to that problem today specifically.

In other words, what was it that happened in their life that made them decide to turn on their computer, go to Google, and search on the term "How to Improve Memory"? Did they forget something important that caused great heartache? Were they studying for a test and having trouble remembering information they need to memorize? What was it?

Both *what* and *why* are valuable pieces of information worth gathering and analyzing, which you'll want to echo back in your marketing.

Now, I'm not going to go into detail about how to code or design a website or Landing Page from a technical standpoint, because there are a number of ways to do it—and a number of online resources that teach how to do so. But this gives you a framework to follow for building a landing page to acquire survey data, if you do not already have an existing email list.

A NOTE about sending paid traffic to this type of landing page: In order to advertise on any advertising network, whether that's Google AdWords, Yahoo/Bing, Facebook, or any other advertising network, you will need to ensure your website and landing page is compliant with the advertising network's terms of service. Oftentimes, these terms can change on a monthly basis (so it's important to be aware of their most current iteration), but here are a few common points that tend to come up consistently from network to network:

- Most networks require creating a more substantial website that extends beyond a single landing page.
- Required pages often include Privacy Policy, Contact Page (with your full company information), Terms & Conditions, Content Pages (e.g., articles or videos which add value to the visiting experience), and, in some cases, a clear explanation as to what you sell and how your business model operates.

This list is certainly not exhaustive, and you should most certainly refer to the actual terms of service of the networks on which you're planning on advertising before running the advertising to your site. But this will give you a starting point if you don't have an existing email list or website, so you can start running your *Deep Dive Survey* and begin gathering market data.

CHAPTER FOURTEEN

Persuade

The Prospect Self-Discovery Landing Page

OVERVIEW: THE LANDING PAGE

Now that we've covered the "pre-funnel" work, the foundational research you perform *before* your prospect ever enters into your "live" sales funnel, let's go through a typical *Survey Funnel* as your prospects would experience it themselves, starting with the first step: Your Landing Page.

> **IMPORTANT:** This landing page is different from the landing page we discussed in the *Deep Dive* chapter. The *Deep Dive Survey* landing page is a temporary step to gather survey data in the absence of having access to an email list you can survey directly. The landing page we'll be covering in this chapter will become a permanent part of your online sales funnel. In other words, this is the first page prospects will land on in your website when going through your Survey Funnel process.

■ ■ ■

MAKING A GOOD FIRST IMPRESSION

Your "Landing Page" is the page you'll drive your online visitors to so they can enter into your sales funnel through your *Micro-Commitment Bucket Survey*, which I'll cover in more detail in the next chapter. In this chapter, we'll be covering the landing page itself, which has a few very important ingredients that will help it perform as well as possible for you, like this landing page here from our RocketMemory™ business:

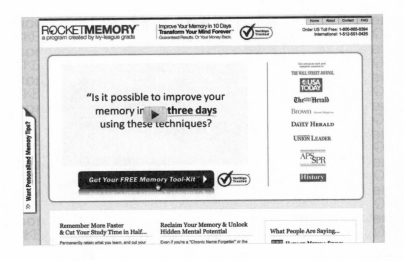

First, *presentation* and *positioning* are key. If you introduce your *Micro-Commitment Bucket Survey* to your audience without teeing up the survey in the right way, your uptake on people actually answering your questions is going to be very low.

It may be obvious, but you do not want to say, "Take this survey so I can learn more about you and I can do a better job of selling you stuff." Instead, your landing page, and how you position your survey, is all about playing "doctor." Because what you'll be doing on this page is *diagnosing* the challenge or problem your website visitor is struggling with, and then *prescribing a solution* to that problem.

Based on all your data from the *Deep Dive Survey*, you'll know which specific challenges, concerns, or problems your market is struggling with. On your landing page, what you're saying is this: *"By asking you a few questions we can help diagnose your problem, give you the solution, and even customize that solution to help your particular situation."*

Keep that in the front of your mind as we discuss the following elements on your landing page. *You are trying to diagnose your prospect's problem and ultimately give them the very best solution.*

. . .

THE LANDING PAGE VIDEO

While in some markets *text-only* landing pages have outperformed landing pages with video, I generally recommend using video because we've found in most markets video outperforms text-only pages. If you are using video, this video is the single most important element on your landing page, because this video is what will convince people to fill out your survey and enter your sales funnel.

The video can either be a "talking head" video or live action, or it can even be text or slides on the screen narrated to audio. Which style you choose will depend heavily on your business model, but I suggest you focus *first* on getting the script right and using whichever video style is easiest for you to execute first. Once the script is right, you can make fancier videos later.

We're going to spend a little bit of time talking about what makes a good *pre-survey landing page video* later in this chapter. But before we do, let's look at the overall page.

• • •

COMPANY BRANDING

One common mistake people make is that they use a large header in order to emphasize their company logo or branding. The problem is that this pushes everything else on the landing page "below the fold," meaning below the bottom edge of your website visitor's screen, where they need to scroll down to see it. It's vital that the most important elements on your page for your visitor are all visible on the screen without having to scroll.

So your site's header should include only a small logo, a tagline for the business or primary benefit, the 1-800 telephone number, and if you have a "trust logo," include that as well. And that's all. At a normal resolution, it should be less than an inch high, like you see here:

To make your landing page look like part of your full website, you also want to have some typical site-navigation elements, such as links to your homepage, about page, contact page and FAQs—which are tucked away and as little distracting as possible.

Your header should be filled with *trust elements*, so that when people arrive at your landing page, their immediate, almost unconscious reaction is, "This is a legitimate business. This isn't just some fly-by-night operation trying to fish for my personal information. This is a custom page, which someone took the time and energy and effort to develop."

When possible, it's worth considering adding logos from any media mentions in which you or your company has been pointed out. These should be actual media outlets in which you've been featured. Only use media in which you or your company has been featured in actual *news stories* (as opposed to paid advertising). You should be prepared to back up any media mentions with proof, and be sure to consult with an attorney before deciding whether it's okay to use any particular media mention.

If you are going to be using media logos, I often like to run them on a semi-transparency, so they recede in the background a little bit. What that does is give you the same positive benefits of having the media logos, without taking away or competing with your primary "Call to Action," which in our case on this landing page is to click the big bold button in the middle of the page and take our *Micro-Commitment Bucket Survey.*

Another trick is to take a step back from your computer, walk about 10 feet away from your computer, and take the "blur test." If you were to blur your eyes and say, "If everything else blends together, what is it that stands out?" You want your primary *call to action*—the big bold button in the middle of the page—to be the one thing that stands out.

· · ·

HEADLINE

Next, you'll want to focus on the headline on your landing page, which is the single most important piece of *written* copy on this page. This headline will either be directly above your landing page video (if you're creating a live action video) or on the initial video frame itself.

One of my favorite constructions to use is to ask a compelling question, such as the one on the RocketMemory™ landing page example:

"Is it possible to improve your memory in just three days using these techniques?"

The reason for phrasing the headline in the form of a question is because it's much more powerful to ask a question like this than to frame the same idea in the form of a statement.

If the headline were to say, "You can improve your memory in just three days using these techniques," it sets off a prospect's B.S. detector—and generates a response of, "Yeah right, prove it to me." Whereas when the headline reads, "Is it possible to improve your memory in just three days using these techniques?"—for most prospects in this market, it generates a response of, "I don't know. Can you? I'm curious. I'd like to know."

Additionally, when you frame your headline in the form of a question like this, the website visitor's brain immediately and almost involuntarily jumps to the conclusion, "Well, I'm not sure, but I'm guessing the way I get an answer to that question is to click the play button on this video, so let's go ahead and do that now."

You're basically telling your prospect that what you're about to demonstrate is possible, and you're showing them what they need to do to learn more.

. . .

FOR THE READERS

Everything below the video on this page is a section I call "For the Readers."

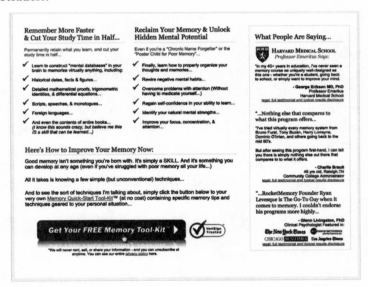

Not everybody likes to watch videos on their computer, and putting some basic text here gives you the opportunity to sell people on taking the survey, in text form. What I also like to include here are testimonials from credible sources and quotations from media mentions, as well as customer reviews.

I also summarize, in two or three very brief paragraphs, the big benefit that people get out of moving forward, even if they don't want watch the video on this page.

Where does the language to describe these benefits come from? It comes from the *Deep Dive Survey* process. And in the case of the RocketMemory™ landing page you see here, that language also comes from actually getting on the phone with some of the prospects who took our *Deep Dive Survey* to understand in a very deep way what benefits they're most interested in. As far as the copy on your landing page, you're just echoing back the benefits you've discovered your market wants in the same language your prospects are using.

Next, let's talk about what's in the video itself.

■   ■   ■

SCRIPTING THE LANDING PAGE VIDEO

For technical information on making videos, there are plenty of guides available online or at your favorite bookstore on the finer technical points of video creation. Technology changes, so it's best to be current.

Instead, what I want to talk about now is the psychology of constructing the script that sells people on taking your survey—and that psychology will never change as long as people are people. When it comes to the outline for your landing page video (that sells people on taking the survey), there are a handful of key points you want to hit. In my experience, the nitty-gritty details of the script fall into place very easily if you hit these points clearly and correctly.

■   ■   ■

THE HOOK

So the first piece in your landing page video is your "hook." A hook is a compelling big idea that simultaneously inspires curiosity and desire in your prospect's brain. "I want to learn more and I want this." You want a juicy hook that really pulls people in. I like to ask it in the form of a question, for the reasons we talked about earlier, to set people up for a big benefit, without setting off their BS detector.

You may be asking yourself, "What's the hook for my business?" Well, that's where you, as an entrepreneur, need to earn your money. In fact, coming up with a juicy hook is *such* an important piece of the puzzle, and it's imperative to really dial this in. When it comes to figuring out your hook, you need something that's unique, that will resonate with your audience based on the research you've done in your market. If you need some ideas on how to come up with compelling hooks, you'll find more information in the bonus section of the *Ask Formula* website. (Note: Bonus Material available at: *http://www.AskFormula.com/bonuses.*)

In our marketing business example, our hook is a concept we introduce called "Your #1 marketing bottleneck."

There is an art to this, more than just a science, because it really takes giving it a lot of thought. It's worth spending some time wracking your brain on the big hook that will grab buyers in your market and pull them into your video.

When coming up with your hook, remember: We're about to be their "doctor". We're about to help people diagnose something in their lives, and we're going to ask them a series of questions to help figure out what that problem, challenge, or undesirable situation is.

Your prospects and your customers have a rough idea of something they're struggling with, whether it's their tennis serve, growing their business, losing weight—it doesn't really matter what it is.

But just like when you go to the doctor and you don't know what's wrong with your body, your prospects have a tendency to think there are an unlimited number of possibilities of things that could be causing their problem.

It's akin to going to the doctor and saying, "Man, doc, I'm feeling tired. I'm putting on weight, my joints hurt, I have a stiff neck, and my vision is a little bit blurred. I don't know what the heck's wrong. I don't know if it's arthritis or if it's something more serious. I don't know what's going on with my body. Help."

Oftentimes, that's the point your prospect is at when they arrive at your site. They don't know exactly what the answer is for their problems. They might not have been thinking about this, but there's something in their life they're uncertain about and they're seeking guidance and help for it.

That's what your job is, that's what we're using this *Survey Funnel* process to help determine, and that's where your hook should come from.

So imagine the doctor saying to the patient, "Time out a second; calm down. Let me ask you a few questions. Let's talk about the joint pain. Is it more of a dull, constant pain or does it come and go in fits and starts?"

"It comes and goes."

"Okay, now let's talk about your fatigue. Are you tired all the time throughout the day, or is it more just in the morning or afternoon?"

"It's in the afternoon."

What we're doing here is asking a series of questions to take those unlimited possibilities in your prospect's mind and try to narrow down what's going on, so we can make our recommendation. We identify the mystery problem or obstacle they might be struggling with.

In our landing page video script we help them see that there are only a finite number of possibilities, and that will give them instant mental relief.

Here is an example of a video opening using my own marketing agency and training business. This structure is extremely simple to substitute with nearly any business, and you can model this script over and over in multiple markets.

"When it comes to your business, is it really possible to double your revenue simply by identifying your number one marketing bottleneck?

*Here's the thing... When it comes to growing your business, there are basically **seven** possible bottlenecks that can hold businesses back from reaching the next level of income. And every business tends to have a **primary** marketing bottleneck, which is the #1 thing holding them back.*

However, the challenge is this: As a business owner with hundreds of different competing priorities, it's sometimes difficult to have enough perspective to identify what that #1 marketing bottleneck is and how to fix it.

Solving this problem for business owners is what my team and I do all day, every day..."

That's a basic example, but let's dissect what I've done there, from a scripting standpoint.

First, I've opened up with the hook or an angle with a big promise of possibility—in this case doubling your business—by solving this problem. Then I've hinted at the fact that there are only a finite number of underlying possible problems that people can run into. To go back to our doctor example, after you describe your list of symptoms, Doc says, "People who come in and see me really suffer from one of five different conditions."

All of a sudden, as a patient, your anxiety levels have subsided considerably because instead of 100 different possibilities, you now know there are only five possible things. That is much more manageable and a lot less frightening.

As human beings, when there are too many possibilities, it makes us extremely anxious. It creates a tremendous amount of uncertainty and stress. It's one of the reasons why, when people are presented with too many choices for things, they end up just not purchasing anything at all.

Basically, it's overwhelming.

And when people have the feeling of being overwhelmed by too many choices, the fight, flight, or freeze response kicks in. Their brain tells them, "You don't have time to make this decision; it's too complicated; let's put it off and move on."

In our script we're saying that's not the case, and so we've relieved that first level of anxiety. They've gone from a limitless number of potential concerns or problems to a finite number, whether it's five or seven or nine or ten (ideally, no more than ten) possible issues. It makes it manageable.

Next, now that we have them captured with our hook, we want to help make them absolutely certain they are in the right place to get help with their problem, now that they know their solution will be just one of a few possibilities.

. . .

IF-THEN STATEMENTS
The next thing I like to include in here is a series of if-then statements.

Here's another example:

If you've struggled to make cold traffic work... if you've struggled with an under-optimized marketing funnel... or if you're launching a new product or business, and you've struggled to build a profitable sales funnel to get that product or business off the ground...then pay close attention, because there's a reason why. And the reason why is because as a marketer, when you've got half a dozen different competing priorities in your business, it's difficult to figure out the #1 biggest leverage point in your marketing to focus on first...

Simply put: It's tough to see the entire picture when you are already inside the frame...

I like to make this if/then section as inclusive as possible because, at this point in your script, your prospect is asking, "That sounds cool, but will this help me?" There are a couple of different ways you can use the if/then construction, but I like to follow up with it right after that juicy hook.

In the example we've been using for my marketing business it would be:

- If you have a marketing funnel but you struggled to make cold traffic work...
- If you have an existing funnel but you're struggling to optimize it...
- If you have a number of different segments in your market and you just aren't sure how to speak to all of them...

To get these kinds of statements, you go back to your *Deep Dive Survey* research, and look for all the broad "themes" as your prospects have described them. If we go back to my *Deep Dive Survey* in this example, the three previous "if" statements were the three broadest themes that emerged.

The "then" part can vary in several different ways. The most basic construction is, "Then this could be the most important video you ever watch, and here's why..." That's the default fallback line you can use if you can't think of a catchier one, and it works great.

Another "then" possibility would be, "Then there's a reason why..." You then go on to explain the fundamental reason why they are suffering from their issues.

These two are basic and workable, but anything can be a "then" as long as it entices the viewer to keep watching more while they discover how to get a diagnosis.

. . .

Promise of the Solution and Reintroducing Another Challenge

The next part of the landing page script is where we introduce the promise of the solution. This is where we get into tying the hook, or the big angle, we came up with at the beginning, and we then bring that full-circle after the if/then piece.

But there is a "trick" we use to keep the viewer in suspense so they keep watching.

We've hinted at the solution (e.g., identifying your #1 Marketing Bottleneck), but then we go back and we reintroduce another challenge. The construction I like to use here is a go-to device you can use for virtually any *Survey Funnel* construction:

Dismissing the option of a "one-size-fits-all" solution.

For example: "The challenge is this: When it comes to identifying what's holding your business back, there is no one-size-fits-all answer..."

Or a different example: "When it comes to choosing a diet, the reason why people struggle is because there's no one-size-fits-all answer for keeping off all the weight..."

It's a universal concept that people will always buy into because it's true. We're all different. All of our businesses are different. Our brains and bodies all operate differently. We are raised to want to believe in our unique individual specialness. You can use that construction in virtually any market, and it's incredibly powerful when you actually *combine* this sales argument with the idea of offering differentiated solutions for each of the major themes you've identified in your market through your *Deep Dive Survey*.

. . .

CREDIBILITY AND PROOF

The next thing we need to get into is credibility and proof.

In your video script so far, you've led with your big concept—your *hook*. You've then given your prospective customer a little bit of hope with the idea that there are only a finite number of possibilities. But then you've pulled away by saying, "But the challenge is there's no one-size-fits-all answer and figuring out your #1 Marketing Bottleneck can be a challenge."

That's the reason why we have this tool here.

(The "tool," of course, being our *Micro-Commitment Bucket Survey*, which we'll be using to "diagnose and prescribe" as we'll cover in the next chapter.)

"But first, if you're like most people, you're probably wondering who am I and why should you pay attention to what I'm about to show you..."

There are different ways you can approach this, but here is a basic and functional structure, which you don't need to change very much. This is where you introduce a few statements about your credibility. Pick the two to three most relevant, compelling data points that prove why people should pay attention to you.

That's the easiest way to introduce yourself. If you have very lofty and impressive credentials, there is even a simple way to claim those credits and accolades without bragging.

For example: "If you're not involved in the markets like sports, satellite television, or alkaline health, then you might not be familiar with the man who has been behind the marketing responsible for creating the number-one companies in each of those markets..."

Or another example: "If you haven't followed football that closely, then you might not realize that the quarterback coach responsible for putting Peyton Manning, Cam Newton, Tom Brady, and Eli Manning into the NFL is a gentleman by the name of..."

Pay attention to the way in which both of those introductions were phrased as compared to declaring, "Hi, my name is so-and-so, the quarterback coach responsible for bringing Peyton Manning, Eli Manning, Tom Brady, and Cam Newton into the NFL..."

When you say it the second way, it sounds like you're bragging, and that makes people raise their defenses. If you present it as a fact they may not know, it feels more like you're just informing them.

The main point here is that you want to introduce some brief elements of credibility, giving viewers a reason why anyone should pay attention to you, without coming across as a narcissistic megalomaniac.

. . .

Presenting the Survey

The next piece of the landing page video script formula is to give them a reason why your survey exists. Why did you make this analysis tool that will help them discover their primary problem? You can make this tie into your expertise that we just shared with them previously.

For example: "What I've been doing over the last 5 to 10 years of my career has involved creating a process I use with every private client who applies to work with me. I ask them a series of questions about their business, which helps me to identify, in just 30 seconds, what the #1 biggest bottleneck is in their sales funnel, and how to fix it. Up until now, my clients paid me $50,000 to $100,000 or more to consult with them and go through this process. What I've done is I've taken that formerly closed-door process and I've developed a simpler free online analysis tool that asks those very same questions. So now you can experience what it's like to figure out your #1 bottleneck and get yourself on a path to fixing it right here, right now."

Let's break down that example: How did the survey come about, and why is it here? (We'll get to the reason why it's free in a moment.) But basically, when it comes to positioning the reason for your survey / tool's existence, a universal "story arc" I like to use that works extremely well (as long as it is, in fact, true) is the following:

The story starts with the expert explaining how they've worked with people one-on-one in person. This can obviously be problematic for serving every prospect looking for help because it takes time, you have to go to a specific location where the expert is located, and it can be very expensive. (That's the setup for why they aren't able to meet with everyone in person and why there is an online solution.)

While this universal story structure won't work for every business, most businesses can use a variation on this theme. For example, it makes sense for a business consultant, for a nutritionist prescribing a diet, or a sports professional teaching people to improve their game. This story automatically makes it completely logical that you would create an online version in order to serve more people.

Say you're a physician, offering your joint-pain diagnosis: "Previously, the only way to work with me in this process was to fly out to my private practice in San Francisco, which is booked up for the next nine months, spend time with me, stay in a hotel, take time off from work, and be away from your family for three or four days. But now you can do it right there in the comfort of your home, and the best part is it only takes about 30 to 60 seconds to complete."

We're taking a personalized one-on-one experience, and we're building it into an analysis tool. When people hear that, they say internally, "That's great, because I don't have the resources and time to go fly out and work with you personally," or, "Ryan, I don't have $50,000 to $100,000 to invest in my business right now to work with you one-on-one, so this reasonable approximation of your process all of a sudden sounds very appealing."

You've juxtaposed it against the alternative, which is expensive and resource-intensive.

> **NOTE:** I know some people may be wondering how to use this formula for selling and promoting physical products. You use it like this...

Imagine you own a purse store, where you sell physical purses. If someone walked into your store and said, "I want a leather bag for my wife as a gift for her birthday but I'm an idiot when it comes to buying women's bags. Where do I start? Help me choose."

As a shop owner or store clerk, what would you do in person?

You'd probably say, "Let's talk about your wife. What kind of bag does she have now? Is it a bag that looks like this, this, or this?"

and you'd show him a very large mommy bag, an in-between sized bag, and a really small bag to help narrow their choices.

Your customer might say, "Oh, it's kind of like the one in between."

"Okay, now how does your wife like to use the bag? Does she keep her stuff in it all the time or is this more of a bag that she would use on special occasions?"

"This would be more of an everyday bag."

"Okay. Talk to me about the things she likes to carry in her bag. Does she carry stuff for your son in that bag, or is it just for her?"

"It's just for her. We have a separate bag for our son when we travel with him."

Whether you sell a physical product, digital product, or some type of service, what we're doing in our survey is asking a series of questions that approximates the experience of what it's like being in person with you, helping the customer choose the solution that's best for them.

WHY FREE?

This universal story also raises a question in your prospect's mind, which you also must answer: "Why are you making it available for free? If your process is so valuable, if your client practice is so booked up, if you are the best-selling leather handbag store on the planet, why are you making this available online for free?"

You need a good reason for that, and there are a number of ways you can justify your tool's existence for free in a straightforward, simple way.

For example: "Now that my practice has reached this point, I am only able to personally help so many people each week. The only way to do more is to expand outside my geographic area and my private practice and begin helping people online. And that's the reason why I've decided to make this tool available to anybody for free."

If you've read between the lines, everything we've done here is setting people up to think, "I'm about to discover something extremely valuable about myself, and this is an otherwise expensive process that I'm getting access to for free. I'd be an idiot not to take advantage of this opportunity."

. . .

FIRST CALL TO ACTION

Once the prospect has been almost mesmerized by the idea of taking the survey (which we know will offer them tremendous benefit because you'll be delivering on your promise), we have to snap them out of it and make them act with our first "call to action." This simply means you directly instruct the viewer on exactly what you want them to do next. In this case, it's to click the link or button to kick-off the *Micro-Commitment Bucket Survey*.

It might go something like this: "So here's what you need to do now: If you're interested or even just curious, here's what I recommend... After you finish watching this video, scroll down, click on the big yellow button that says XYZ, and then answer the five easy questions that pop up. Once you've answered those questions, enter your name and email, and on the other side you'll get an instant video, walking you through your #1 marketing bottleneck, along with how to fix it, minutes from this very moment..."

Simply adjust the details and specifics in the above piece of script to make it your own, and that's your first call to action.

. . .

THE TAKE-AWAY

In marketing terms, a take away is when you warn the prospect that if they walk away from the offer on the table, you will "take away" some component or even the whole offer.

In our landing page video script formula, the take away is typically a variation on the following:

"The only catch is this. Because this tool is typically only something that I give access to my private clients, I haven't decided how much longer I'll be making this tool available for free. So here's what I recommend..."

This is a very simple take away and it's honest; the prospect feels like it makes sense and they do feel the pressure but don't feel pushed or coerced. Your goal here is to "inspire people into action." Remind yourself you have a duty and responsibility to help your prospective customers, and the first step in that process is to make sure they complete this survey and do it now.

After this, we introduce our second (and final) call to action. For example:

"Go ahead and do this now while you're on this page and thinking about it. Simply click on the button below, answer the questions that pop up and I'll see you on the side with your #1 funnel bottleneck and how to fix it, minutes from this very moment."

And that's the end of the video.

One final question you may have is "How long should these videos be?" The answer is "long enough to cover the important parts, but short enough to keep it interesting." Generally, I like to keep these videos between 90 seconds and three minutes. That's usually enough to convey what you need to convey. The shorter the better, with three minutes being the absolute maximum I'll go for.

As we discussed earlier, you might even consider testing a "text only" version of your landing page against a version with your video. Again, in some markets, I've found a simple text-only page is not only sufficient to inspire visitors to take your survey— but it actually outperforms the video version.

That's basically the formula in a nutshell, from the opening "hook" headline, all the way through that final piece, the two "calls to action", and the "take away" in between.

CHAPTER FIFTEEN

Segment

The Micro-Commitment Bucket Survey

OVERVIEW

In this chapter we're going to be covering the next step in the *Survey Funnel* process—the *Micro-Commitment Bucket Survey*. This is what your prospect sees initially when the video starts to play.

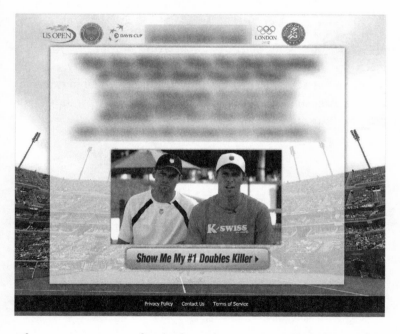

After your prospect is finished watching your Landing Page video, and they click on the button to start your *Micro-Commitment Bucket Survey*, the first step in your survey will look something like this:

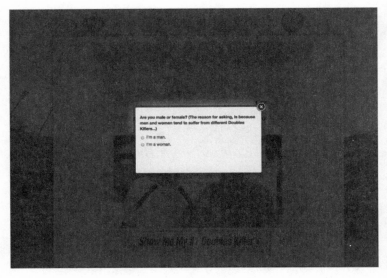

(Note: This example was created using *http://www.SurveyFunnelSoftware.com.*)

In other words, you'll ask your prospect to answer a series of multiple-choice questions, one question at a time, until they ultimately reach the final step in your *Micro-Commitment Bucket Survey* where you ask them to provide their name and email in exchange for the diagnosis, recommendation, or customized solution you promised in your Landing Page video.

■ ■ ■

How to Come up with Questions
In this next section, we'll cover how to come up with your *Micro-Commitment Bucket Survey* questions, how many questions to ask, and the order in which to ask them. To do this, we'll be going back to the *Deep Dive Survey* data we organized and sorted into different themes.

■ ■ ■

Condensing Categories
From our *Deep Dive Survey*, here is our MS Excel file with all the data.

If you remember, our goal is to cover 80% of the market with three to five different buckets. In this particular example, as you're about to discover, I was able to cover 73% of my market with my top four buckets, and this was close enough to my target to leave me satisfied. Let me describe what those four buckets ended up being, so you can understand the context for what we're going to get into.

• • •

FOUR MAIN PROBLEMS

It turns out, after doing an exhaustive analysis of the data, that people coming to me for help were experiencing four main problems:

Problem #1: The first theme I saw was people having multiple products they're trying to sell to their market without having a good way to match the *right* product or the *right* message to the *right* segment of their audience.

Problem #2: The second theme I saw was people who were struggling to make paid, cold traffic convert. Sometimes they made joint-venture traffic and internal warm traffic work a bit, but they weren't able to make cold traffic work very effectively.

Problem #3: The third theme I saw were people who had existing funnels but wanted to fix them, optimize them, improve the conversion rate, add backend elements, or do a better job with product sequencing. Basically, they wanted to improve the funnel they already had.

Problem #4: The fourth and final theme I saw were people looking to get into new markets or launch a new business and needed to build an entire funnel from scratch.

Those were my four buckets. I did not make them up, and they were *not* what I originally had expected. But the data was clear.

Now, using this information, I'll walk you through the process of coming up with the questions for your *Micro-Commitment Bucket Survey*, which, in our example, is going to lead people into one of these four buckets or categories.

$$\bullet \ \bullet \ \bullet$$

CREATING QUESTIONS

When you're creating a *Micro-Commitment Bucket Survey*, there are three categories of questions that you want to think about:

- Your "Grease the Wheels" Question
- Your "Personalization" Questions
- Your "Segmentation" Question

To illustrate and explain these question types, I'll use the actual questions my team and I decided to include in the *Micro-Commitment Bucket Survey* in our example.

$$\bullet \ \bullet \ \bullet$$

QUESTION #1: FULL-TIME OR PART-TIME

In every *Micro-Commitment Bucket Survey*, your first question should be what I describe as your "Grease the Wheels" question. This is a very simple, low-threshold question you want to ask people that's (a) useful for you to know the answer to; and (b) designed to get them to start taking the survey.

It needs to be such a simple question that someone can answer the question without stopping to think about what about what the right answer is for them.

I'll give you a couple of examples...

Typically, in most markets, the first question I like to ask—if relevant—is, *"Are you a man or are you a woman?"* The reason I ask that is because people can answer the question with virtually 100% accuracy, without having to really think about it. The reason why I want to ask a simple, low-threshold, low-commitment question like this is to get the ball rolling, to get the process moving.

It's helpful to think about this question in relationship terms. If asking for someone's name and email is like reaching out for a hug or kiss... then this initial "Grease the Wheels" question is like waving "hi" from afar. You don't want to scare people off.

This is where the whole *Micro-Commitment* concept comes into play: When you ask someone to make any sort of change or take any sort of step—the brain perceives that change as a threat. A perceived threat fires off warning bells in an area of your brain known as the limbic system, which is responsible for, among many things, *your fight-or-flight response.*

When you ask someone to take a step that's too large and too threatening online—like providing their name and email address as the *first* thing you ask them to do when they come to your website—it sets off those same limbic-system warning bells. The result is often that people leave your website without opting in— or they provide a fake name and email address.

However, by asking someone to first answer a simple multiple-choice question (especially one that's extremely simple and non-threatening), you can create "action-taking momentum" *without* eliciting the fight or flight response in your prospect's brain. And the result? Far more people are willing to provide their name and email address, and oftentimes gladly so.

In our example, the first question I decided to ask in our *Micro-Commitment Bucket Survey* as our "Grease the Wheels" question is the same question we used in our *Deep Dive Survey*:

1. Which of the following best describes you?
    ( ) My Internet business is my full-time income...
    ( ) I also have a separate "day job"...

It's simple, easy to answer, and only has two choices—A or B— and those two choices don't overlap one another. You're either male or female. You either have a day job or you don't.

. . .

QUESTION #2: BUSINESS TYPE

Next, you want to move to the second category of questions: your "personalization" questions. You'll be using the answers to these questions to "personalize" your marketing messaging. A typical "personalization" question I like to ask is a person's age (i.e., thirties, forties, fifties, etc.) whenever relevant.

The reason why is because we'll be capturing these responses, appending those responses to a person's database record when they opt in to your email list, and referring to them later on—in, for instance, your email follow-up messages.

For example, knowing a prospect's age, you can use "merge fields" in your email. If you're in a health market, you can write things like, "If you're in your [age], then you might've noticed your body has started to slow down..." Here [age] is replaced with "fifties" or whatever age demographic your prospect falls into.

You can do this by passing survey responses to your email follow-up system. While it sounds very technical, there are several ways to accomplish this. One of the ways is to use the *Survey Funnel Software* I've mentioned, which we've developed for this very purpose, and which integrates with virtually every email follow-up software on the market. You can learn more by visiting *http://www.SurveyFunnelSoftware.com*.

The second reason for asking "personalization" questions is so you can use the information to laser-target sub-segments of your market for future promotions or product offers.

As we discussed earlier in the book, this gives you the ability to target, for example, "women in their forties and fifties" if you sell a menopause-related product. The applications are virtually endless, but the point is this: *By asking several "personalization" questions, you're able to gather useful information about your prospect so you can introduce better-matched products and services both immediately and in the future, as well as customize your marketing language so that it speaks directly to who they are.*

In our example, the first "personalization" question I ask—the second question in our *Micro-Commitment Bucket Survey*—is *"Which of the following best describes your primary business?"*

After gathering data from the *Deep Dive Survey*, I refined the multiple-choice options to include:

2. Which of the following best describes your primary business?
　　( ) I'm a biz owner. I sell my own products and/or sell as an affiliate.
　　( ) I'm a marketing consultant who helps biz owners.

I decided to eliminate four categories I had included when asking this question in our *Deep Dive Survey*:

- I sell products as an affiliate.
- I'm a copywriter.
- I'm an employee of a company.
- Other.

I eliminated the separate "affiliate" option and combined it into the primary "biz owner" category, because the "affiliate" numbers were small (<5%) and the vast majority of those respondents also sold their own products, so I was able to consolidate those two categories.

I eliminated the "copywriter" option because the numbers were also very small and, based on the feedback I received, the sub-group of copywriters who represent potential prospects in my business also consider themselves to be "consultants." So I'm able to combine those two categories together.

I eliminated the "employee" option because I'm not terribly interested in selling to employees of companies; they're a relatively small segment to begin with, and they're not really the market I'm after. The *Deep Dive Survey* results confirmed that it was a small segment, and one I could ignore.

Finally, I eliminated the "other" category because the majority of these respondents actually did a combination of "selling their own product" and "consulting." What I've done here is focus on what makes the biggest difference in terms of how I communicate with someone in my marketing:

- "Whether someone *sells their own products* or they're a *consultant*."

Wherever possible, I'm looking for *80/20* opportunities like this to reduce the number of potential survey answers to present to a prospect. Generally speaking, all things being equal, the fewer options you present, the easier the question is to answer, *and* the more likely your prospect will answer the question and move onto the next question in your survey.

• • •

QUESTION #3: TRAFFIC SITUATION

The next question I decided to include is one that gives me a sense for a prospect's traffic situation:

3. In terms of your [Internet business / consulting practice], which of the following describes your traffic situation?

( ) I'm currently getting thousands of visitors to my website each month...

( ) I'm struggling to get more traffic...

The reason for this question is that one of the demarcation lines I discovered in the *Deep Dive Survey* was a marked difference between businesses who were generating significant traffic, and those who weren't. These two sub-groups largely suffered from non-overlapping issues. I wanted the ability to "tag" a prospect according to their traffic situation so I can introduce them to products and services related to generating website traffic, which are appropriate based on their situation.

> **NOTE:** You'll notice part of the question is phrased in [brackets]. One of the things you'll want to do when designing your questions is make it a point to reference a prospect's answers to their previous questions where appropriate. This is important for a few reasons.
>
> First, it conveys that the information your prospect is providing is actually being used to take into account their situation. Just like if you were having a conversation with someone in person, repeating things they've told you about themselves demonstrates that you're listening to them. This, in turn, encourages them to tell you more about themselves. Similarly, in the extensive testing I've done, we've found that when you "customize" the questions like this, more people complete the survey.
>
> Secondly, in some cases you may actually want to use "conditional logic" to show different questions (or multiple-choice options) based on how a person answers previous questions. For example: If you sell a fitness product, and someone answers "male" to question Number 1, in your second question you might ask,

"As a man, which part of your body are you most looking to improve? a) Your belly, b) Your chest, or c) Your arms. Whereas if someone answers "female" to question Number 1, you might present a different set of options, which might include "thighs" and "hip area."

If you're wondering "How do you technically implement all this?" there are several technical solutions on the market that do elements of what I just described, as well as the software my team and I developed for this very purpose: *http://www.SurveyFunnelSoftware.com*, which allows you to do everything we just discussed.

. . .

QUESTION #4: EMAIL LIST SITUATION
The next question I settled on is as follows:

4. Which of the following describes your email list situation?

( ) I have a large email list with thousands of subscribers I'm able to mail to...

( ) I have a small (or non-existent) email list...

This is relevant information for me because it tells me what approach that person will need to take with respect to conducting their *Deep Dive Survey* when it comes to implementing the *Survey Funnel* process in their business. This, in turn, will impact my messaging, and even what products and services I might introduce to them.

. . .

QUESTION #5: BUSINESS SIZE
For the reasons we've already discussed, I also want to know the size of a prospect's business.

5. Roughly, what's the size of your [Internet business / consulting practice] in terms of Gross Sales?

( ) < $100K

( ) $100K to $499K

( ) $500K to $999K

( ) $1M+

While my company and I do lot of high-level work with larger businesses, the majority of those clients are introduced to us through referrals and other channels. The *Micro-Commitment Bucket Survey* we're building here is designed to target smaller businesses through cold traffic.

You'll notice again that I've consolidated the number of options with an 80/20 focus in mind. In this case, these four buckets cover 86% of my market based on the results from our *Deep Dive Survey*.

. . .

QUESTION #6: THE SEGMENTATION QUESTION

The final question in this survey is my "Segmentation" question: the question I'll be using to funnel people into different buckets.

Now, when you're going through this process yourself you might ask yourself, "What dimension should I use to segment my prospects? Should I choose one variable? Should I choose *multiple* variables? Should I do it based on *gender*, *age*, on *business size* or *type*? What should I use?"

My answer to that question is that it's going to depend on the specifics of *your* business and what is most important when it comes to customizing your marketing messaging and the products and services you introduce to each of your different segments.

Oftentimes, segmenting by demographics is less effective than segmenting based on the nuances of the situation, challenge, or problem your prospective customer is looking to solve. You'll often see demographic patterns and trends that emerge, but segmenting around a core issue—and customizing your messaging based on *that*—is generally more effective than picking a demographic variable.

. . .

To give you a better sense, let's take a look at my *Segmentation Question* in our example:

> 6. The [Internet business / consulting practice] clients I work with who are doing [less than $100K / at least $100K / at least $500K / at least $1M] per year, who are [getting

decent traffic / struggling to get traffic] and who have a [large email list / small or non-existent email list] tend to struggle with one of several marketing challenges. Which of the following is your biggest challenge right now?

( ) **Selling to Multiple Sub-Markets:** Within my market, there are multiple sub-groups of people with different needs and wants, and I need a way to match the right message, products, and services to each sub-group.

( ) **Making Paid Traffic Convert:** I need a way to convert cold traffic, so I can afford to buy traffic to scale my business instead of relying on JVs, affiliates, and organic SEO.

( ) **Fixing an Existing Funnel:** I have an existing marketing funnel, but it's not converting like I want. I specifically need help with better lead capture, sales copy, email follow-up, and back-end product sequencing.

( ) **Entering a New Market:** I'm launching a new business or product line right now, and I need to set up a brand new marketing funnel from scratch, and I don't know where to start.

( ) **None of the above:** Honestly, none of the above really describes my situation.

So how did I arrive at this question and these options as my *Segmentation Question?* Let's dissect what we're looking at step-by-step starting with the question.

What I've done here, using a prospect's responses to their previous questions, is customize how the question reads to take into account their situation.

For example, if a prospect sells their own products, is generating between $100,000 and $499,000 in revenue each year, is getting decent traffic to their website, and has a large email list, the question would read: *"The Internet business clients I work with who are doing at least $100,000 per year, who are getting decent traffic and who have a large email list, tend to struggle with one of several marketing challenges. Which of the following is your biggest challenge right now?"*

Let me draw your attention to a few things: Notice how I said, "doing at least $100,000 per year" instead of "doing between $100,000 and $499,000."

Of those two options, which sounds more natural and the way you might speak if you were having a conversation with someone in person? The first option.

What I'm trying to do here is to phrase my questions in such a way that they represent how I would have this conversation with someone in person, naturally, in a very non-robotic, non-formulaic way.

In fact—and this is important—you almost want to *understate* the fact that you're using this customization in your questions. You want to insert phraseology that feels *natural*.

It's the same thing with the "traffic" component to the question: When I say "getting decent traffic" or "struggling to get traffic," this is very colloquial. It's natural.

And this benefits your prospective customers as well: If you have something of value to offer that can change their lives in a positive way, then you want to use the same language you might use if you were standing in front of that prospect and helping them in person.

. . .

In fact, that's the *big idea* here

The questions you ask in your *Micro-Commitment Bucket Survey* should mimic the experience someone might have if you were asking them a series of questions in person to get to know them a little bit better and recommend a solution to them.

. . .

This is the crux to the entire *Ask Formula* concept...

If someone raises their hand and says, "I need help," in person, we'll naturally ask that person a series of questions to get a better sense of what they're looking for, what they've tried, and what they're struggling with.

But online, this almost never happens.

So as a result, there's a tremendous amount of inefficiency in the way business is transacted online. The website visitor loses out because they feel like they haven't been heard and perceive the solution you're offering isn't for *them*. Thus they leave frustrated, without a solution. The merchant loses out because they lose out on a potential sale.

If scale weren't an issue, you might connect every single website visitor with a live salesperson who can take them through this process. But that's not simply *feasible* for most businesses that operate in scale.

This *Micro-Commitment Bucket Survey* approximates this experience in a way that's both scalable, and where everybody wins.

Now that we've covered the *question* in our *Segmentation Question* example, let's move onto the potential answers I've settled on, so you can understand the rationale behind those options.

You might be wondering: Do all prospects see the same five options irrespective of how they answer the previous questions in the survey? The answer is, that depends.

In our example, the answer is "yes." The reason why is because, based on the results of my *Deep Dive Survey* (coupled with my knowledge of the market and my customers), there are essentially four major challenges people are looking to solve when they come to me:

- Selling to Multiple Sub-Markets
- Making Paid Traffic Convert
- Fixing an Existing Funnel
- Entering a New Market or Product Line

It doesn't matter if the business is doing $100,000/year or $10M/year in revenue; the problems are generally the same. That said, the *specific solutions* I might present to each of those businesses might be different.

For example, I might suggest a Training Course or Coaching Program for the first business that is likely in the category of "having more time than money." In other words, it's likely they would rather do the work themselves in order to save money. And I might direct the second company toward our Sales Funnel Implementation Services on the agency side of the business, because they are more likely to want to hire the professionals to do the implementation for them.

I won't get into all the technical details behind how to set this up because there are several ways to do it programmatically and it will depend on the technology you're using in your business. But, essentially, what you can do is capture the demographic variable (in our case, "business size") and append that information to your sales page URL, so that the $100K business and $10M business see two different variations on the same sales messaging. The messages might be virtually identical, except for the specific product recommendation that you make.

After your prospect has answered your *Segmentation Question*, you have two options: You can either send them directly to a customized product sales page, or you can first send them to a name and email capture page, which enables you to capture all the survey information in your email follow-up system, so you can communicate with your prospect both immediately and over time.

Generally, I recommend the latter unless there is a specific reason not to ask for their name and email address. The reason why is because, while you might turn away a certain number of prospects with this step, your ability to communicate with that prospect through email in a very targeted way (which we'll be covering in detail later in this book) more than offsets any revenue you might lose initially from prospects who decide to leave your website at the name/email opt-in step.

One last thing to mention before we move on to the next section, where we'll be covering what to do *after* someone has entered their name and email and submitted the survey, is this: In our example, you'll notice that I've chosen to add an "Other" option on our *Segmentation Question*. I've done this as a "check and balance" to make sure the other options I've presented cover at least 80-90% of my market. If I see more than 10% (and certainly if I see more than 20%) of respondents choosing "Other," then it tells me I might need to go back and rethink the options I've chosen.

This is an optional step, and not required when designing your final *Segmentation Question* in your *Micro-Commitment Bucket Survey*.

Now, let's move on to the Post-Survey "Same Visit Sale" webpage—the *next* step in the *Survey Funnel* process.

CHAPTER SIXTEEN

Prescribe

The Post-Survey Sales Prescription

OVERVIEW

Just to recap what we've covered so far: Your prospects will first come to your Landing Page, where they will see a short video explaining why they should take your *Micro-Commitment Bucket Survey*. There, they will click a button to start the survey, answer the questions that pop up, enter their name and email (in most cases), and click a button to submit.

From there, after submitting their survey responses, they're going to land on your Post-Survey "Same Visit Sale" Page, which is what we'll be focusing on in this chapter.

On this page, you're going to be doing two different things:

1. You're going to offer valuable education to your prospect for free. More specifically, you're going to educate them by addressing the concerns and situation they described in the survey. This is where you'll be playing doctor, where you explain to them what their *symptoms* mean, and how to *solve* their particular problem.

2. This education piece will transition into an *offer*. More specifically, after you present some value-added information for free, you're going to then present your prospect with the paid solution you recommend based on what they've told you about their situation. Generally, your goal is to generate a sale here on this initial visit to your website—hence, this page is called the Post-Survey *Same Visit Sale* page.

There's an art to providing both pieces of useful education to the prospect, so they feel like they've gotten tremendous value from taking the survey, and then still leaving them "wanting more" and motivating them to invest in your paid solution. There are nuances to this part of the process that are important to get right.

So let's cover what the *Same Visit Sales* page looks like and what it should include in more detail, as well as how your sales message should be presented.

■ ■ ■

SAME-VISIT SALES PAGE
Here's an example:

I've blurred out the headline, for competitive interest reasons, but I just want to show you what this page looks like. There are a couple different things going on here. We've got the video (what you're looking at is actually a paused video, not a static image). We've got a headline. And below the video is all the sales copy that's on the page.

When someone first lands on this page, the only thing they'll see is the video itself and the headline above it. The price, the Add to Cart button, and sales copy below are all hidden. They only become visible at the point in the video where you introduce the paid solution you're suggesting.

The reason for that is simple: When people first land on this page, you want the content of your video (and your prospect's attention) to be 100% focused on the personalized feedback you're offering based on the *results* of their survey.

If we use the analogy of the doctor's visit again, this is the point when you, as the doctor, are explaining what your prospect's symptoms mean and how their experience differs from people in other situations; you're beginning to walk through the possible options they have to solve their particular issue.

What you're *not* doing is rushing to recommend surgery and explaining how much that costs. That will come later.

You want to first provide value and build trust. You want to demonstrate that you have an intimate understanding of their situation and what they're struggling with. You want to show them—through that demonstrated understanding—that you know what they're going through. And when you do that, using all the feedback you've received from your *Deep Dive Survey*, you're going to produce a reaction in your prospect's mind: *"Oh my gosh, it's like you read my mind. It's like you read a page out of my diary. It's like you know exactly what's going on in my life."*

And once you've done that, their next reaction is going to be: *"What do you recommend that I do about it?"*

But you have to get to that point *before* you introduce your paid offer.

■ ■ ■

PAGE LAYOUT

You'll notice the page is just on a white background. The focus is entirely on the message in your video, with as few distractions on the page as possible.

■ ■ ■

EXIT LANDER

Not every visitor will be interested or in a position to watch your entire video from start to finish. Some visitors will be short on time, in a rush, or might not like consuming information through video. For this reason, you'll want to create an "Exit Lander"—a text and graphical summary of the offer you're making.

If someone starts to "exit" your sales video page—either by clicking the "back" button on their browser, closing the tab they're in, or even by expressing "behavioral intent" and moving their mouse outside the browser frame—you'll want to present them with the option to read a "quick summary" of the offer you're making.

This page should be relatively short—and not a word-for-word transcript of your video. My team and I have done a significant amount of testing here, and have found long, word-for-word transcripts under-perform summary pages, which include:

1. The Big Benefit: What's in it for your customer when they purchase?
2. The Offer: What exactly are you selling?
3. The Bonuses: What free extras / bonuses are you including?
4. The Price: What discounted price / special deal are you making available?
5. Guarantee: What money-back guarantee / risk-reversal are you providing?
6. Reason to act now: What's the deadline, limited quantity, or reason to act now?

• • •

CONSTRUCTING THE SCRIPT

The single most important part of your *Same Visit Sales Page* is the script for your video. To cover all the important nuances of scripting video sales copy would require another 300-page book, so I've provided a Resource Guide with my list of recommended resources. (Note: Bonus Material available at: *http://www.AskFormula.com/bonuses.*)

That being said, I want to spend a moment discussing the overall structure of your script, in terms of the main "story arc" you want to follow in the context of the *Survey Funnel* framework to give you some high-level direction.

. . .

PROBLEM, AGITATE, SOLUTION

The most adaptable, universal script formula I like to use in virtually every *Same Visit Sale* video script where appropriate is called "Problem, Agitate, Solution." This is where you introduce the prospect's problem, reinforce the severity and urgency of that problem by "agitating" that problem in your prospect's mind, and then finally introducing your solution to that problem.

The reason you want to do this is because the problem you're helping your prospect solve could just be one of 50 things causing anxiety in your prospect's mind. What you need to do is agitate the problem to *intensify* it in such a way so that everything else disappears.

The *most important* thing you need to do is help your prospect focus on solving the problem they came to you for, and solve that problem now. Here is the structure to use to do that and help guide you in crafting your sales message:

STEP 1: ACKNOWLEDGE THEIR SURVEY SUBMISSION

The first thing you want to do is acknowledge and thank your prospect for taking the survey: It can be as simple as, "Thank you for taking the survey." You might want to acknowledge their intelligence, or their motivation.

For example, "Clearly, improving the sales conversion in your business is something you really care about, and it's a really smart decision you've made by spending the time to focus in on trying to figure out what the #1 marketing funnel bottleneck *is* in your business."

STEP 2: PROVIDE YOUR DIAGNOSIS AND LABEL IT

This is where you identify and, ideally, attach a "label" to your prospect's situation. Again, if we use the analogy of playing doctor, this is where you say, *"Based on everything you've told me about your situation, the challenges you're facing, your #1 problem right now is what we call..."*

In our example, my language here would read: "Based on what you've told me about your business, where you're at currently, and what you've told me you're struggling with right now, your #1 Marketing Bottleneck is something I like to call the Cold Traffic Curse. Let me explain what that is, and what it means for businesses in that situation..."

What I've done here is applied a "label" to the diagnosis I've made by introducing the term "Cold Traffic Curse." (NOTE: This is just one of the possible diagnoses from our example *Survey Funnel*. The actual diagnosis a prospect receives will depend on their answers to the *Micro-Commitment Bucket Survey* questions.)

By applying a "label" to their situation (particularly one your prospect hasn't heard before and one which induces curiosity), the immediate reaction in their mind becomes:

"What *is* the Cold Traffic Curse, and what does it mean exactly?"

In our Problem, Agitate, Solution framework—this is the "Problem" phase.

STEP 3: EXPLAIN WHAT THE DIAGNOSIS MEANS

In this next step, you'll explain what the diagnosis means and how it affects your prospect. This is the "Agitate" phase in our "Problem, Agitate, Solution" framework. There is a temptation to keep this section brief and rush to talk about your solution. This is a common mistake.

The key in this step is to accomplish three main objectives:

1. Demonstrate that you *understand*. Show that you know exactly what the prospect is going through by describing their "symptoms" or their pain in such vivid detail that their reaction becomes, "Wow, it's like you can see inside my head, like you're living in my home, and know exactly what I'm thinking and going through." Use your feedback from the *Deep Dive Survey* and your own knowledge of the market to demonstrate your understanding.
2. Demonstrate the *urgency* and *severity* of their problem by putting it under the spotlight. This problem needs to become the single most important thing in their life to solve, and to solve now.

3. Demonstrate that you *care*. As the expression goes, "People don't care how much you know, until they know how much you care." Before introducing your solution, demonstrate your genuine desire to help your prospect solve this problem in their life. This needs to be genuine. It needs to be real. This is how you segue into the fourth and final step of your sales message: the solution.

STEP 4: Explain Your Recommended Solution

After you've introduced the *problem* and sufficiently *agitated* that problem, then it's time to introduce your solution. Here you'll want to present your solution in the context of other solutions they might be aware of and considering. Again, if we use the "playing doctor" analogy, you want to introduce the various options your prospect has based on their circumstances, and make your *recommendation*—along with *why* you recommend that option over all the other possibilities at their disposal.

When you introduce your paid offer as your recommended solution, like in the summary option you'll provide, you'll want to cover all the following elements in this section of your video script:

1. The Big Benefit: What's in it for your customer when they purchase?
2. The Offer: What exactly are you selling?
3. The Bonuses: What free extras / bonuses are you including?
4. The Price: What discounted price / special deal are you making available?
5. Guarantee: What money-back guarantee / risk-reversal are you providing?
6. Reason to Act Now: What's the deadline, limited quantity, or reason to act now?

One element you might have noticed to be absent from this list is "Testimonials"—also known as "Success Stories" or "Case Studies." I want to mention a note about Testimonials.

I've done extensive testing around including vs. excluding testimonials in video sales scripts. My team and I have tracked video engagement extensively and have found that reading customer and client testimonials verbatim in the context of a video sales message generally results in a significant drop-off in video viewership. In other words, if you start reading client testimonials verbatim in your sales video script, viewers tend to pause or leave the video in large numbers.

So the solution to this is as follows: *Present the full written testimonial on screen to demonstrate its completeness and authenticity, but only read one or two lines or a summary from that testimonial when delivering the actual sales message.*

Here is a fictitious testimonial as an example: *"Hi, my name is Mary and I've been trying to lose weight for the past three years, and nothing has seemed to work. After having my second child, and gaining an extra 37 lbs. following the pregnancy, I just haven't been able to get back to my pre-baby weight. I had literally tried everything until finally stumbling on your website seven months ago. I've been following your recommended plan ever since, and I've already lost thirteen lbs. Thank you so much!"*

When integrating into your video sales script, it might be read as follows: *"If you're wondering what kind of results this program has delivered, well, consider Mary, who lost thirteen pounds after struggling to lose weight after the birth of her second child..."*

(This would be read while presenting the full *written* testimonial on the screen at the same time.)

Lastly, while this should not be considered a substitute for legal advice, be sure to comply with all relevant regulatory bodies and advertising guidelines, by including all necessary testimonial-results disclosures when informing your prospect of the results achieved by other clients and customers.

Profit

The Profit Maximization Upsell Sequence

OVERVIEW

In the previous chapter, we covered the *Post-Survey "Same Visit Sale"* Page. Again, your goal is to generate a sale on a prospect's *initial* visit to your website.

However, generally speaking, this initial sale is *not* where the majority of your profit will come from. In fact, it's not uncommon to simply break even, or perhaps even *lose money* on this initial visit in order to generate a customer.

But once you've generated a customer, the *real* profit comes from what else you sell to that customer both initially and over time. This is where the *"Profit Maximization Upsell Sequence"* comes into play.

■ ■ ■

PROFIT MAXIMIZATION: ALL AROUND US

There is a certain fast-food restaurant, which supposedly invests $1.97 in advertising on average per customer, just to get that customer to drive up to the drive-through in one of their restaurants. In other words, the millions of dollars spent in advertising generate customers at a cost of $1.97 each.

At this particular restaurant, the most common initial "front-end" purchase is a hamburger, which generates on average $2.08 worth of profit, nearly all of which is used to cover that $1.97 advertising cost. In other words, this initial front-end purchase generates $0.11 in profit per customer.

So how does this restaurant stay in business?

As soon as someone is invited to add French fries and a soft drink to their order—and perhaps even one of their famous dessert items, the profit per customer soars from $0.11 to $1.13. In other words, profit literally increases *ten times*, simply by asking the customer, "Would you like fries and a drink with that?"

This is what the *Profit Maximization Sequence* is designed to do. And because it's so critical to achieving massive success online using the *Survey Funnel* model, here are a few key components of this sequence.

■ ■ ■

PROFIT MAXIMIZATION SEQUENCE EXPLAINED

One of the most challenging things in business online is convincing someone to take out their wallet and spend money with you. There is a tremendous amount of inertia you must overcome, both mental (e.g., "Do I *really* want to spend money on this?") and physical (e.g., "Do I *really* want to leave my comfortable couch, walk across the house to find my wallet and credit card, and walk all the way back here? Or should I just do this later?").

However, once someone has made that first purchase and they're in a buying mindset, they're much more likely to spend *more* money right then and there. Understanding this process, you can (and should) take advantage of that fact for the mutual benefit of both you and your customer.

Having a customer spend more money with your company is naturally beneficial to *you*, but this is also the absolute *best* time to introduce additional related products and services that can help the life of your customer, which they might not otherwise purchase outside this critically important "buying window."

This is where the *Profit Maximization Sequence* comes into play. Here's how it works:

Immediately after your prospect makes the initial purchase, you will present them with one or more "one-click upsell" opportunities, where they can add additional products or services—presented one at a time—by simply clicking a button, and without having to re-enter their payment information (hence the "one click" in "one click upsell"). These offers are presented *after* the initial sale is made so as to not jeopardize the initial sale.

Now, it's important that these additional offers *enhance* the initial purchase in some way, and don't create the reaction, "Wait, I thought the first thing I just bought was supposed to solve that problem?" Otherwise you will (rightfully) create a bad taste in your new customer's mouth.

Instead, there are three frameworks I like to use—and which work well when executed properly—when it comes to your *Profit Maximization Sequence.*

. . .

Upsell/Cross-sell Framework #1: Selling Value

This is the most basic, straightforward framework. In this first framework, you are upselling more of what the customer just purchased but at the same or a better-discounted price. If you're selling a single tub of protein powder—a 30-day supply, for example—this is where you might offer three more tubs (an additional 90-day supply) at a discount, and with free shipping when purchased all together. This framework works well with consumable products—a second copy/unit could be ordered for a friend, family member, coworker, or employee.

. . .

Upsell Framework #2: Speed & Ease of Implementation

In this second framework, you're upselling customers a faster, easier result—based on the problem they came to you for help solving.

For example, if you sell a gym membership online for people looking to get into shape, you might upsell customers into a 30-day boot camp, to get into shape faster, with more one-on-one support. If you're selling an online course on how to integrate surveys into your marketing, you might upsell people into a software solution that does most of the heavy lifting. If you sell furniture, you might sell a white-glove installation and assembly service.

Again, the name of the game here is speed and ease of implementation. This framework works well if you can offer coaching, consulting, software, or done-for-you services that help your customer achieve the result they're looking for—faster, easier, and with less work on their part.

. . .

UPSELL FRAMEWORK #3: FUTURE-PACING A PROBLEM THEY DON'T YET HAVE

This third framework is the most complex, but it can also be the most powerful. Let me explain how it works: What you're doing here is introducing a "good" problem they don't yet have, but *will* have after getting results from your initial product, and which will need solving. You then make the argument as to why they should invest in a solution to that *new* problem now, which simultaneously reinforces their confidence in the initial purchase they made.

Let me illustrate with an example: Let's pretend you sell a salary-negotiation course, which helps people negotiate higher salaries—anywhere from 20-50% higher than what they're currently being paid.

Using this framework, your upsell might be something like this:

After getting that 20-50% raise, and seeing your first paycheck with that new number, if you're like most people your initial reaction is going to be, 'What should I do with this excess cash?' One of the biggest mistakes people make is buy 'nicer stuff' and immediately raise their cost of living. Instead, there is no better time to get ahead financially, and take a portion of that raise and invest in your retirement. But in order to avoid the inevitable temptation of spending that extra money, you need to be prepared. You need to have a plan. And you need to have that plan going into your salary negotiation before you see that first new paycheck, and temptation takes over. You need to know exactly how you're going to invest a portion of that salary increase before that first big check is direct deposited into your bank account—so you and your family can finally get ahead financially. This is why I want to tell you about a complimentary program we offer which helps you determine how much of your raise you should invest, and where you should invest it. It's called....

· · ·

What we've done here is introduce a *new* "good" problem the customer doesn't yet have—i.e., excess money to invest following a successful salary negotiation—and presented an argument of why this problem should be solved now rather than later. We've also reinforced their confidence that the initial purchase will produce the desired result, by putting forth the assumption that the salary negotiation will be successful.

· · ·

THE "ALMOST AS GOOD" DOWNSELL

Whether you use Framework #1, #2, or #3 (or some combination thereof), what happens if your customer declines to "upgrade" their order to include your one-click upsell offer?

This is where the "Almost as Good" Downsell comes into play.

First, it's important that you price your one-click upsell offer in such a way that you have "room" to offer a less expensive alternative should your customer decline the opportunity.

This is critical: *there needs to be a contrast between what they want and what they can afford.*

Oftentimes, customers might be interested in your one-click upsell, but the price is just a little more than they want to pay, or there isn't a burning, urgent enough desire to upgrade their order to include the initial upsell offer.

If your customer says "no thanks" to your initial offer, you can offer what I describe as the "Almost as Good" *Downsell* version of that offer (it's essentially framed as "80% of the results at 20% of the cost.")

If you're offering a full-blown salary surplus investment course, you might offer a "fast-track" version at 20% of the cost. If you're offering an additional 90-day supply of your protein powder—three additional tubs, and your customer says "no thanks," you might offer one additional tub and still upgrade the order to free shipping, when the answer is "yes."

Again, the name of the game here is "Almost as Good" (80% of the benefit, at 20% of the cost).

. . .

One-Time Offer

One last point to consider: Generally, no matter which framework you use, I like to make the "one-click" offer something that's only available right here, right now—and not something the customer will be able to take advantage of later.

When you do this, it enables you to make products and services available to your customers at a price that you normally wouldn't be able to offer—e.g., by shipping multiple products together and passing the shipping and fulfillment cost savings to your customer, etc. However, if you *do* express that this is a one-time offer, it *truly* must be a one-time offer. It needs to be honest, genuine, and authentic. When you do this, stick to your word—it creates long-lasting benefits between you and your customers for years to come.

CHAPTER EIGHTEEN

Pivot
The Email Follow-Up Feedback Loop

OVERVIEW

So far we've covered everything your prospects experience from the time they first hit your Landing Page, complete your *Micro-Commitment Bucket Survey*, view your *Same Visit Sales* Message, and even experience your *Profit Maximization Upsell Sequence* if they become customers. All of this can potentially happen within minutes of first visiting your website. But not all sales are made that quickly.

And for that reason, following up with prospects (non-buyers) and buyers via email is an essential part of the *Survey Funnel Strategy*. In fact, depending on the market, I will pick up anywhere from 25% to 75% of our sales from email. This is important. When it comes to converting website visitors into customers I've found that most marketers give up *way too soon*. Only a small fraction of website visitors are positioned to purchase on the first point of contact with your website. Depending on what market you operate in, if you're able to convert anywhere from 1-10% of cold traffic into customers on that same visit sale, you're doing *very* well.

And to put that *another* way, even if you are able to convert 10% of website visitors in to customers, what that means is at best, 90% of all the time, effort, energy, and *money* you invest in generating that traffic is essentially a waste—*unless* you follow-up with those individuals. The *real* secret to taking your business to the *next level* is knowing how to convert a portion of the 90% of non-buyers into paying customers. And because this is an area I see so many businesses fall short, we'll be spending a significant amount of time in this chapter focused what emails to send to website visitors who do not purchase from you on that same visit sale.

The other major benefit of using email in your *Survey Funnel* is the fact that it gives you a constant feedback loop to help you iterate, optimize, and *improve* your marketing funnel by listening to, and incorporating, the constant feedback you receive from your market, often in *real time*. This is something almost *nobody* does, and it's one of the *easiest* ways to improve the performance of your marketing.

There are two different email sequences we'll be covering in this chapter—one for buyers, and one for non-buyers.

There is some overlap between the two sequences. And because we'll be covering the non-buyer sequence first, it doesn't make sense to repeat in detail the components that carry over to the buyer email sequence, when we get to that section. So, know that while the buyer sequence section is *shorter*, that does not mean the buyer email sequence any less important. In many ways, the buyer email sequence represents one of the lowest hanging fruit profit opportunities for most businesses because you're communicating with individuals who have already spent money with you—and thus are more likely to spend more money with you, if you simply communicate with them in the way you're about to discover.

Also, there is some flexibility in terms of how many emails you send out in each sequence and several sequential variations you can use. But to keep things simple, I'm going to walk through my email sequence that consists of *three series of four emails* each, so 12 emails are sent to the buyers, and 12 to the non-buyers (if a non-buyer becomes a buyer mid-stream, they're moved from the non-buyer sequence to the buyer sequence, and will not receive the otherwise remaining non-buyer emails.)

By using the *Survey Funnel* Software (*http://www.SurveyFunnelSoftware.com*) in tandem with your current email autoresponder program, you can customize each of these emails using merge fields or dynamic text blocks based on how an individual answers the *Micro-Commitment Bucket Survey* questions. You can even add email subscribers to completely different email sequences by using the *Segmentation Question* in your *Micro-Commitment Bucket Survey* to add people to different lists.

I'll outline each of the series of emails for you and tell you what goes into each individual email, but first let's look at some general (but slightly unconventional) tips about what makes these emails different than a typical promotional email you may get from a company you've interacted with.

. . .

GENERAL, BUT SLIGHTLY UNCONVENTIONAL EMAIL TIPS

In any email, generally the first thing the reader sees is the subject line. Entire books have been written strictly about writing subject lines that get opened. But to keep things simple, I'm going to show you one technique that's extremely powerful which appeals to your prospect's curiosity, and closes what we describe as an "open loop"—an incomplete thought on which the brain seeks closure.

A simple way to take advantage of this motivating force is to make the subject line of your email into an incomplete thought. This makes the recipient curious enough to open the email and complete the thought.

For example, a subject line might read, "Where there's a will there's a..."

Even something cliché like that will tickle the reader's curiosity and they will open the email to complete the thought.

In the emails themselves, I also train people to write short, punchy sentences. Unlike most "corporate" emails, these should sound casual and conversational, like a message you would send to a friend, rather than a professional contact. (Remember in my story I told about how influential the writings of the late Gary Halbert were to me—this is where I learned so much and where his writing brilliance comes into play.)

This conversational style of writing is to make the recipient feel comfortable reading the email right away rather than mentally classifying it as an advertisement and ignoring it. Your emails should *not* read (or even look) like promotional messages.

The last general tip applies to all emails you send your prospects and customers. Generally, you should always "condition for the click," meaning that every email needs to have a link that leads elsewhere.

Whether it's a link to more information or to a purchase page doesn't matter as much as always having something to click. We want to condition our readers to respond to us and click the links we send them, so we make that a part of every message.

Those simple tips will not only make all your customer and prospect emails more effective; they are also key to the two *Survey Funnel* email sequences we are covering here in this chapter.

Firstly, let's begin with the Non-Buyer or Prospect sequence.

■ ■ ■

Non-Buyer Email Sequence

This sequence is to be sent to the people who filled out our *Micro-Commitment Bucket Survey* but who did not buy the immediate offer we presented to them. These emails are meant to keep the readers engaged and rescue the sale by gently reminding them that they are interested in what you have. (And remember, these people can become buyers at any time and will automatically kick over into the buyer sequence when this happens.)

In the first series of four emails to non-buyers, we warm them up by giving them exactly what we promised when they completed the survey.

■ ■ ■

Email #1: The Results Email (actually, all *Micro-Commitment Bucket Survey*-takers get this whether they bought or not)

The first email your prospect will receive will deliver the results of their survey responses. This email will contain a brief explanation of what those results mean, and how they can apply those results to solving their problem.

The goal of this email is to bring them back to our sales message and get them to consume it again, but it's framed around the delivery of those promised insights and advice that their *Micro-Commitment Bucket Survey* responses have generated.

. . .

EMAILS #2, #3, #4: THE STORY SERIES—THE SOFT SELL APPROACH

The next three emails are called a "story" series. These are meant to be casual, story-based reminders that, again, pull your non-buyer back to our core sales message by getting one "story" type email per day over three days. Depending on the market, this might be a specially constructed story broken into three pieces over three days. And it can also just be three individual stories if that is simpler for you to create.

A very simple way to create these is to choose your three strongest points from your sales message and use one for each email, but retell it from a firsthand perspective.

For example, if one of your key points is the quality of your product over that offered by your competitors, you could tell a story about how a person might suffer if they mistakenly got a lower quality solution.

You don't have to become a literary genius to tell these stories; remember that we are aiming to come across like a friend, so just sharing a simple anecdote like you would relate to a buddy at the water cooler is the ideal tone.

And don't forget, each of these emails should tie in and link back to your sales message again. We want them to fully consume it if they didn't before, or reconsider it if they didn't take you up on the offer the first time.

. . .

SALES ACCELERATION SERIES (EMAILS #5, #6, #7, AND #8)

The second series of four emails is designed to turn up the heat, in a way. If the results and the story series didn't get them to buy, it should have at least warmed them up.

If they didn't unsubscribe, it's safe to assume that we simply haven't given them a sweet enough deal or an urgent enough reason to buy now. So for the whole series here, we are going to modify our offer to lower the barrier to the sale and create urgency to buy in the process.

How we do that is going to be different depending on the market and product, but I want to stress that we are *not* offering a further discount; we just want to lower the threshold of commitment.

This can potentially mean offering a one-dollar trial period with the full amount being billed later. It can be a split-pay option to spread the cost out over a couple of months. It can also be a "just pay shipping" offer, where the customer covers the cost of shipping and is billed the cost of the product at a later date if they choose to keep it.

When my team and I design and write these series, whatever the client can manage as the best possible deal is the one we will push for, as long as we avoid devaluing the product by discounting it further.

By creating this "twist" on our offer, it creates a valid reason for us to keep emailing non-buyers about the same product, and it allows us to create a new deadline to take advantage of this new, lower-threshold option.

Another key part of this *Sales Acceleration* series is that we are going to try to aim at a few different target buyers. In my experience, there are four main types of buyer psychology in every market.

The *Sales Acceleration* series is all about giving each of those different "types" a message that speaks directly to that mindset to give them the nudge they need to make a buying decision.

■ ■ ■

EMAIL #5: THE URGENCY EMAIL

The first email we send in this series following the three-email story series is an "Urgency" email. This message is more direct and promotional than the previous ones. Our goal is to remind them of the urgency and time limitations inherent in our offer.

We want to stress the importance of making a decision now, before it's too late. It helps to highlight the savings and additional benefits involved in this special offer.

The "Urgency" email is designed to appeal to your *impulse buyer type*. In their day-to-day lives, people with this mindset often feel rushed or overloaded, and presenting our offer this way gets their attention and makes purchasing feel like a relief. They enjoy "jumping" on opportunities like this and some will even thank you for bringing the opportunity to their attention.

• • •

EMAIL #6: THE FAQ EMAIL

The next email is what I call the "FAQ" email, and it's designed to appeal to the more *analytical, logical mindset*. People who think this way usually resist any offers that have an element of uncertainty or any unanswered questions.

The trick is that, a lot of times, they don't mentally form these questions in order to ask them. So even though they want to buy, they just leave a big question mark over your offer and put it off.

So in this email, we focus on filling in all the details we can about the buying process, but present them in a question/answer format. "What do I get in the offer?" "How much does this special offer cost vs. the regular price?" "What bonuses are included?" "What kind of guarantee is there?"

Providing these details will eliminate the unanswered questions in your logical buyer's mind and will make them feel comfortable and confident in finally taking you up on your offer.

• • •

EMAIL #7: THE TESTIMONIAL EMAIL

The next email features personal stories from previous customers and clients who have used your products and services. This "Testimonial" email is meant to appeal to the *people who respond best to stories from other people*.

Whereas your logical buyers would like to hear about the technical specs of a car they want to buy, these folks want to hear stories about how fun it is to drive through the countryside with the top down.

And so we use your previous customers as a shortcut to give these prospects stories about using your products and getting results. This will help them imagine using the product themselves, and getting the same kind of results.

All they need is a little fuel for their imagination, and there is no better fuel than the real-life experiences of others who already love your products and are happy to buy from you.

■ ■ ■

EMAIL #8: THE "LAST DAY" EMAIL

The final email in this series is what I call the "Last Day" email, and it is meant to give a last little push for the *procrastinator mindset*. Some people are wired to wait until the last possible minute no matter what.

The trick is that people who think this way frequently miss out on things because they wait too long. So by sending them a reminder that your special offer is now expiring and it's their last chance, you're doing them a favor.

They are happy because they already wanted your offer, but their mindset makes them put it off and they never make the time to follow up. But because you reminded them, they won't miss out like they normally do.

■ ■ ■

FEEDBACK LOOP SERIES (EMAILS #9, #10, #11, AND #12)

This last series of emails we send to our non-buyers is called the *Feedback Loop* series because it presents them the opportunity to interact with us.

With the information we get from those interactions, we will do two things: get one more chance to close the sale on this offer by tweaking our messages, *and* get in a position to make them our next offer, which we will let them suggest.

At the end of this series, we essentially restart the *Survey Funnel* process all over again with a new product offering—and we can continue like this virtually forever, by stringing together *Survey Funnel* after *Survey Funnel*—one right after the other.

. . .

EMAIL #9: THE "DO YOU HATE ME?" SURVEY EMAIL

Unlike the previous emails in this non-buyer sequence, this email isn't about attempting to close the sale. This email actually drives the reader to fill out another survey: The *Do You Hate Me Survey* that we introduced earlier. This is a one question, open-ended survey to determine why people didn't buy.

This somewhat shocking email/survey gets its name because we jokingly ask if the reader hates us. Because we gave them our best product at our best possible deal, but they simply didn't buy. We want to find out why.

The key to this email is to ask specific but leading questions to let them know what kind of answers will be most useful to you. The email might read like this:

> *Did we not do a good job of explaining something? Did we not do a good job of touching on a specific hot point that matters to you? What's the single biggest reason why you've decided not to work with me? Was it something I said, or didn't say, OR do you just hate me? :-) Please click on the link below and tell me "What was the #1 reason why you decided not to try XYZ product / service?*

The "hate" part is tongue-in-cheek, and the thought behind suggesting they might hate you, even as a joke, is that they probably don't hate you at all. People feel an urge to respond because they are uncomfortable having a negative emotion like hatred attributed to them. In fact, this somewhat perhaps unexpectedly shocking approach, spurs non-buyers to leave detailed, thoughtful answers because they want you to know that they don't hate you at all.

Now we are going to use the information we gather in this survey in three places.

First, when non-buyers provide us with their unaddressed objections, we will use this feedback to constantly tweak and modify our sales video and landing page. Next, we will also address these new objections in our FAQ email we discussed above by continually revising that email over time. And, finally, we can (optionally) take those objections and use them to create a live webinar where our product experts will get on a group call with these prospects and address their concerns head-on.

If you decide to go that route (which is highly recommended) then you can set it up in your next email.

• • •

EMAIL #10: THE RE-OPEN / WEBINAR EMAIL

In this email, in response to the feedback received above—and the fact that there were some questions you didn't completely address—you announce that you are re-opening your best possible offer from your *Sales Acceleration* series. The reason for doing this, is that you will have never covered every possible question *perfectly*. There will always be another objection you didn't think of, something you communicated that was misunderstood, and your marketing will always confuse or stifle some potential buyers.

So almost as a penance, you create one last opportunity for those folks who felt left out. This email lets them know you are doing that, and will tee up your next email, which is another FAQ message, this time focusing on the feedback we received from the *"Do You Hate Me?" Survey*.

If you have chosen to do the live webinar I suggested, this email is where you invite your subscribers and tell them how to register to attend. This webinar is basically a reading of the objections uncovered from the *Do You Hate Me? Survey* and overcoming them, as well as an opportunity to field any live questions from your attendees.

After you've recorded this live online event *once* you can adjust your automated email sequence to send future subscribers to the recording. In other words, you only have to actually conduct this Q&A webinar live *once* after which, you can direct people to watch the recording of it. The process will work almost the exact same way with a recording once you have created it.

• • •

EMAIL #11: THE FAQ / LAST DAY EMAIL

After we announce the reopening of our best offer, and we optionally conduct our live objection-busting webinar, we send out a text version of that material. It is very similar to our previous FAQ email; we offer questions and answers to the objections we collected, and we give the explanations required to eliminate them for prospects who had them.

This is our last attempt at making this specific sale, so we want to give it our best effort, and, of course, we remind them that this will be the last possible day to get the same best deal we initially created for our *Sales Acceleration* series.

■ ■ ■

EMAIL #12: THE PIVOT SURVEY EMAIL

The "final" email in the *Feedback Loop* series and our overall non-buyer sequence is where you set things up to "pivot" in one of several possible *different* directions. This final *Feedback Loop* email contains the *Pivot Survey* we introduced earlier. The idea behind the *Pivot Survey* is that if this initial offer was simply not quite right, you are giving people the opportunity to "pivot" or *choose* which direction to go next.

First, in this email you acknowledge that despite your best possible offer, the previous product deal was simply not for them. But you appreciate their time and attention, and you still want to help them. Then, you present them with several options for what they can do next. Typically, I recommend starting with 3 options. These options should correspond to different products or services you might offer—but will be presented as they relate to your prospect and the benefit they convey.

For example, your *Pivot Survey* email might read:

I understand that the XYZ product wasn't quite right for everyone. I appreciate your time and attention, and I'd still like to help you. So we have several options as to where we can go next. Which of the following best describes what you're most interested in covering next:
( ) How to do X
( ) How to do Y
( ) How to do Z

*Choose the option you'd like to focus on next, and we'll
shift gears and begin covering that subject in more detail....*

The first time you run the *Pivot Survey* by email, you can present
the survey as an open-ended question (like the *Do You Hate Me
Survey*) if you're not sure what options you should present, gather
feedback over time, and then *use* that feedback to come up with
your multiple choice options.

Alternatively, if you're confident that you know based on the
feedback you've already received from your *Deep Dive Survey* and
Do You Hate Me? Survey, you can present the survey as a series of
multiple choice options from day one.

Once you identify the most popular of your suggestions,
the permanent version of your *Pivot Survey* email should be set
up with "choose your own adventure" links, which add people to
one of several *different* auto-responder sequences and send people
to one of several *different* webpages, depending on which option
they selected. The way you do this from a technical standpoint
will depend on which email auto-responder program you use, but
generally speaking you'll be using some form of automation links
to facilitate the redirection.

As far as where you send people *after* they click on one of
the options you've presented, my team and I will initially use the
click data—i.e. how many people *click* on each option—to determine which topic is most popular. From there, we'll start with the
highest-priority topic and construct a brand new *Survey Funnel*
for that particular topic. Once we've created the *Survey Funnel*
for that topic, we'll set things up so that when a prospect clicks on
the link for that topic—the link will direct them to the *Prospect
Self-Discovery Landing Page* for that particular *Survey Funnel* and
simultaneously add them to the non-buyer email sequence for that
particular topic.

We'll then go down the list like that until we've created a
Survey Funnel for each of the *Pivot Survey* options presented. So,
by the time we're finished if a prospect clicks on "How to do X",
they'll be sent to the *Prospect Self-Discovery Landing Page* for the
Survey Funnel that focuses on "Topic X." If they click "How to do

Y", then they'll be sent to the *Survey Funnel* for "Topic Y." And this is the approach we use to "string together" *Survey Funnels* one after another, giving prospects the ability to "choose their own adventure"—or weeks and months into the future in a way that consumers often love—and which is highly-profitable.

Now let's take a look at the *Buyer Sequence*.

• • •

BUYER SEQUENCE

Just like the previous non-buyer sequence, this will consist of 12 total emails, comprising three series of four emails each. Many of these will be extremely similar to the non-buyer sequence, so we will mainly cover the differences.

The main difference is obviously that this sequence is mailed to people who bought the offer that came after the survey. Our goal with this sequence is to get them to use what they bought (consume) and get positive results from what they purchased from us.

But it's also designed to initiate and close *another* sale based on how much they enjoyed what they already got from us. Let's start with the first series.

• • •

EMAIL #1: WELCOME EMAIL

This email is very simple and consists of simply thanking the customer and welcoming them to the fold. We tell them how to get what they purchased, what to expect, and remind them why it was such a smart purchase. If it involved digital downloads, we provide instructions on how to get those. If it involves a physical product being shipped, we tell them what to expect as far as shipping times and what the package will look like.

This email can be brief. The goal is just to keep them excited about their purchase and to create a little bit of expectation by telling them you have some good things coming soon to their inbox.

. . .

EMAILS #2, #3, #4: THE CONSUMPTION SERIES

Much like the "Story" series we emailed to non-buyers, this mini-series can tie together across multiple messages or each can stand alone.

What we are trying to do is make sure the buyer is actually opening and using or consuming whatever they bought. If they don't use it, they won't get the results, and if they don't get the results, we can't call them satisfied customers.

Again, this will vary widely depending on what you sell, whether it's a physical or digital product, and the length of the delivery timeframe. But here are some general ideas for consumption emails:

One idea is that you can create a message focused around the "most important thing" they need to do first when your product arrives. This gives them a small goal they can easily accomplish, but serves to get them moving once they take that first step.

Another idea is to create a series of "exercises" for them across multiple emails, where you tell them not only what to do first, but what to do next, and what to do after that. This is essentially bringing them deeper into your product and getting them to apply it step-by-step if they need the help.

One last idea is to tell them how to get the most out of their purchase by suggesting tweaks or add-ons that go beyond simply using it. This not only gives something useful to the people who are already consuming what they bought, but for people who have put it off, it gives their imagination fuel for what they could be doing if they just get started.

Whichever route you decide to go, a natural consequence of actually using your product is that they go from a "beginner" to an "advanced" user. And once they become more advanced, they have new problems and needs that emerge. You are in an excellent position to assist with these new problems.

. . .

The Upsell / Cross-Sell Series

This series is very similar to the *Sales Accelerator* series you send to non-buyers, but instead of focusing on the same product, you simply introduce them to a new upsell or cross-sell offer.

Ideally, this would be a product that is suitable as a "next step" for people who are successfully applying the product they already bought.

They will have a perfectly natural desire to advance if they are getting the results you promised, and you are essentially getting in front of that desire and offering to help, without them even needing to think to ask or start looking elsewhere.

Other than being a different product or offer, this series is basically identical in structure and function to the *Sales Accelerator* series, where you will create and send four messages.

■ ■ ■

Email #5: The Urgency Email

This email creates a limited-time, "best" offer on the proposed product, which captures the excited impulse buyers who are ready to buy immediately.

■ ■ ■

Email #6: The FAQ Email

This email preemptively answers any unspoken questions and objections your prospect might have about making this new purchase. Again, this helps the analytical, logical buyers make their decision.

■ ■ ■

Email #7: The Testimonial Email

This email shares true first-person experiences from existing customers who have gotten great results by using the product you have on offer. This appeals to people who put more value on stories than on logistics.

. . .

EMAIL # 8: THE LAST DAY EMAIL

This email simply reminds all your buyer types that this is the last day to get the limited-time offer on this upsell, which is, of course, cheaper than they can get anywhere else.

Now let's take a look at our final buyer series.

. . .

FEEDBACK LOOP SERIES

Once more, this series is going to be extremely similar to the one we did for the non-buyer sequence, with minor differences.

The key difference being that this series is going to refer to the Upsell offer we just made, rather than the main product they already bought.

It presumes this is sent only to the people who did not buy the upsell you offered above. Just like in the non-buyer sequence, the objective of this series is to solicit feedback from non-buyers that you can use to convert them one last time, and tweak your offer sequence to better convert new subscribers in the future.

In brief, the four emails for this series are as follows.

. . .

EMAIL #9: THE "DO YOU HATE ME?" EMAIL AND SURVEY

This email asks readers to tell us why they did not buy the upsell item presented, in an effort to uncover hidden objections we can better address.

. . .

EMAIL #10: THE RE-OPEN / WEBINAR EMAIL

This email is used to re-open our best deal on the upsell item and offer to host a live group webinar to address the newly uncovered objections head-on to help close the sale.

. . .

EMAIL #11: THE FAQ / LAST DAY EMAIL

This email pulls the best material from our survey results and objection-busting webinar to eliminate any lingering doubts in potential buyers. We also remind them that the deal ends today, so they have to decide right away.

. . .

EMAIL #12: THE PIVOT SURVEY EMAIL

This is where we acknowledge that our best offer on the upsell simply wasn't for them, and we ask them to pick an option for what they are most interested in next. We present the options we know we can deliver, and use their feedback to choose what our next funnel will promote.

> **NOTE about Evergreen Automation:** After going through each of the email sequences for non-buyers and buyers, you might be wondering, "How do you automate these email sequences in such a way that preserves real deadlines? How do you take into account the *Do You Hate Me?* email feedback if you are running these emails as automated, evergreen sequences? And what tools or technology do you need to make it happen seamlessly? Once again, that special bonus section (which is available to verified readers only) can be found at: *http://www.AskFormula.com/bonuses*.

Just like with the non-buyer sequence, once your reader has reached the *Pivot Survey* in your email sequence, it simultaneously represents the last step in your initial *Survey Funnel* and opens the door to the first step in your next *Survey Funnel*, setting you up to string together multiple Survey Funnels one after another...

. . .

Now that we've reached the last step in the *Survey Funnel* process, since we've covered a lot of ground up until this point, let's recap what we've done, and where we are.

If you remember, our first step was to *Prepare*, and conduct our *Deep Dive Survey*. Second, was to *Persuade* and construct our *Prospect Self-Discovery Landing Page*. Third, was to *Segment* with our *Micro-Commitment Bucket Survey*. Fourth, was to *Prescribe* with our *Same Visit Sales Prescription*. Fifth, was to *Profit* with our *Profit Maximization Sequence*. And finally, our last step was to *Pivot* with our *Email Follow-up Feedback Loop*.

Now that we've covered the *Ask Formula* methodology and the entire *Survey Funnel Strategy* in detail, let's look at a few case studies of businesses that have used the *Ask Formula* in their businesses, and the type of impact it's had on their growth.

CHAPTER NINETEEN

Case Study #1
Tennis Training—
Zero to $250,000 in 6 Months

THE CHALLENGE

By the end of April 2013, the product called *ServeKillers*, created by the PTR Certified Professional Will Hamilton, had reached a sales plateau. Will's company *Fuzzy Yellow Balls* (FuzzyYellowBalls.com) was at a pivotal point in its history. Fuzzy Yellow Balls, or "FYB," as it's known, was a new and innovative website wherein tennis players from across the world could come to learn how to play tennis online for free, discuss the sport, and socialize. The content was unique and very exclusive—with professional instruction taught by pros like former #1 ranked player in the world, Pat Rafter and the all-time winningest doubles tandem in ATP history, Bob and Mike Bryan.

Will packaged some of his technology and tennis strategy into an online training product called *ServeKillers*. *ServeKillers* helped tennis players understand why their serves were not up to par, or what was "killing" them, so to speak. At first, sales were great and membership in the program was growing, but then things began to slow down.

Although FYB was set up using a product-launch model and had been relying on warm JV affiliate traffic with great success, Will realized that the company didn't really have the systems in place to send paid cold traffic consistently to an offer and have that offer convert. He wanted a way to scale the business up very rapidly, which led him to Ryan Levesque's *Ask Formula* and more specifically, his *Survey Funnel Strategy*.

The Implementation

In early May 2013, Will was introduced to Ryan after he came recommended from another one of Ryan's clients. After hearing about the potential of the *Ask Formula*, Will was extremely interested, though he was initially skeptical. However, since Ryan had worked in other sports areas and had been so successful, Will believed it was likely that success could be duplicated for himself as well. He decided to commit 100% to seeing if the *Ask Formula* would work.

FYB dove head on into the *Survey Funnel Strategy*, and implemented it start to finish, using every strategy, concept, and email that Ryan and his team developed. Will implemented the *Deep Dive Survey* to find out what his market was really thinking, and Ryan and his team used the data to script all videos and email copy.

In the end, from all the somewhat unexpected survey feedback Will received from his list, Will came up with *four* major buckets in his market. The *Survey Funnel Strategy* was completely implemented and totally integrated into his business model.

The Outcome

With all the components in place, including the landing page, the video sales letter, the bucket surveys, and follow-up emails, *Serve-Killers* was re-launched again in mid-2013. They added a new touch to the video by introducing former #1 ranked player in the world, Pat Rafter, as the main spokesman with Will in the video.

After the video, the new system carefully guided web visitors through a series of questions and at the end, showed them a different video customized *exactly* to their situation based on their answers, addressing their unique concerns. It also guided them down the funnel to making the purchase of the *ServeKillers* product.

In the first week of its launch, ServeKillers generated $25,000 in income from the single product.

That launch was so successful that they quickly created a second *Survey Funnel* to sell another product called "DoublesKillers."

In the first six months, the DoublesKillers product alone generated another $250,000 for the company and brought in 3,500 new customers.

FYB was officially off the revenue plateau where it had been stuck for so long. They now successfully drive a substantial amount of cold paid traffic for their lead generation, enjoying a much more profitable conversion rate. Both products continue to be wildly successful, and Will now uses Ryan's *Survey Funnel Strategy* to launch every single new product FYB releases, including three new training programs slated to hit the market later this year.

CHAPTER TWENTY

Case Study #2
Water Ionizer Market—
$750,000 in 5 Days

THE CHALLENGE

The water ionization market is highly competitive and filled with skeptics and misinformation. This is the environment in which Ross Bridgeford created a fairly successful online business in 2010 called Live Energized (*liveenergized.com*). Live Energized offered a variety of health products, not the least of which was the flagship product, the $2,000 water ionizer filtration system for home consumer use.

In this tough market, customers must be given a lot of education, proof, and information in order to convert into buyers—a process that historically took place with consumers one-on-one. When prospects understand all the intricate details, they're usually eager to sign on the dotted line. Ross's challenge was figuring out how to duplicate this kind of education and one-on-one salesmanship as closely as possible online in scale, by overcoming objections and offering proof elements throughout the buying process.

Although revenue was coming in before Ross began working with Ryan to implement the *Ask Formula*, it was labor-intensive to keep the business at that level. He had to repeatedly promote the business, running campaign after campaign. He knew he was emailing a lot of people and suspected that he wasn't speaking the right language because they weren't responding. The promotions had a sort of one-size-fits-all approach and he knew some people would be left out but he wasn't certain how to solve the problem.

The Implementation

When Ross heard about Ryan Levesque and the *Survey Funnel Strategy*, he was hopeful this could help him in his business. He hired Ryan and his team, and they started working together and strategizing on how to proceed.

The type of funnel they decided on was not a total implementation of the *Survey Funnel Strategy*. It did not present cold or warm traffic prospects with a sales video followed by a popup saying "Take this quiz to find out what would be best for you," then leading them to the logical conclusion offer based on those answers.

Instead, they created a *hybrid* funnel.

Ryan and Ross started developing this unique sales funnel by conducted some initial fact-finding *Deep Dive Surveys* sent to the buyers and non-buyers from previous promotions on his list.

The surveys uncovered insights Ross could never have imagined, including some amazing "Aha!" moments.

For example, originally Ross had presumed people were coming to his website looking to alkalinize their water and make it better, but what he found out from the surveys was that people were more motivated by their *fear* of what was in their tap water.

This completely changed the first half of the funnel and the whole "story arc," which was really the whole approach he had been taking.

This survey feedback was also used to hone the language for the videos that were to be the centerpieces of the new funnel, which Ryan and his team were designing.

From the *Deep Dive Survey* data, Ross and Ryan identified trends among the hyper-responsive survey-takers. They decided to target their videos toward the people who were most likely to buy, and the language within them addressed the objections and fear that prospects might have while also hitting hard on the benefits.

As they continued setting up this funnel, they waited to finalize each piece of video content based on the feedback they were getting from the first video—literally creating the sales funnel in real time to incorporate up-to-the-minute survey information.

The videos were 70% to 80% there, but they were not finalized until the feedback was collected and analyzed. This method helped craft the message to the exact questions and desires of the prospects.

It also gave Ross and Ryan the opportunity to create additional informational PDFs, addressing specific additional objections and relevant questions. These were displayed and downloadable underneath each video. Each piece of video content was finely honed to perfection before releasing the next. It was a careful and thoughtful process.

In the feedback, many people said they wanted to see Ross actually using the ionizer in the kitchen and instructing them (the third video). To illustrate, here is the list of the types of videos they created for this unique water ionizer sales funnel launch in March 2014:

- Video 1: A sort of "Shock and Awe" video showed prospects what's actually in their tap water and bottled water. It set the stage for saying "You've got a problem and you've got to do something—you HAVE to do something."
- Video 2: "Your Options" video showed prospects the pros and cons of products currently on the market, giving unbiased explanations of each one, showing the expense of each product and how it works, and then ending with a type of teaser for what was coming in the third video.
- Video 3: "Instructional" and teaching video showed Ross testing the ionizer and explaining how to do everything. It was much more instructional and entertaining as well.
- After viewing the third video, prospects were shown the offer and given five days to purchase.

The Outcome

Since Ross and Ryan had built the videos and the funnels with feedback loops and consultation with customers, it seemed complete and they thought they had covered all the bases. And apparently they had.

The *Ask Formula* sales funnel for the Living Energized Water Ionizer launched in March of 2014. *In a period of just five days, the Ask Formula funnel generated $750,000 in sales.*

In fact, in that initial five day period, Ross had to stop selling because he had completely sold out the manufacturer's worldwide supply of the product—putting the product on worldwide back order for several weeks! This *Ask Formula* sales funnel generated four times more revenue than Ross's previous best performing launch sequence, sending to the same size list in June of the previous year.

Ross became so confident with the results that he started sending paid traffic to the funnel in June of 2014 and stopped having to promote his business so hard. The "evergreen funnel" he had set up with Ryan was doing all the hard work for him. He continues using this recurring launch model to this day which generates a six-figure monthly revenue stream, and is enjoying serious financial success.

In fact, because of his positive experience with the *Ask Formula*, Ross has decided work with Ryan and his team to build out complete *Survey Funnels* for multiple new product releases, including his seven-day alkaline cleanse, an alkaline weight-loss product, two alkaline recipe books, and more.

CHAPTER TWENTY-ONE

Why

The Reason for Writing This Book

There you have it. The *Ask Formula* spelled out in its entirety—everything you need to apply the *Ask Formula* in your business, and use it to take your business to the next level.

Okay. Now that we *have* covered the entire formula and methodology, if you are like some people, you may be wondering the reason what I wrote this book and the reason for giving away the entire formula like this.

You might be wondering why someone would *give away* what's essentially their entire "secret family recipe"—something that's taken years to develop and quietly made them *millions* in the process (and which continues to make millions) in the pages of a book available to the general public like this for the entire world to copy and use for themselves.

Well, I'll tell you this: Many people advised against writing this book. Many people said I should keep my formula quiet. That I should continue to profit from it myself. But as you may have learned from reading a little of my story, there are some experiences along the twists and turns of my journey that have had a profound and lasting impact on me.

You see, I really did come close to dying a few years ago. And I have to tell you, when you come to terms with your own mortality like that, it changes your perspective on life. It makes you think about things like contribution, legacy, and *impact*.

Which leads me to the reason why I *did* decide to publish this book—in spite of all the people who suggested I shouldn't.

Now, don't get me wrong—it does not elude me that this book will have a significant commercial impact on my business. That it will generate significant demand for things like our software, coaching programs, and agency services. In fact it already has. But I have an even bigger—no extraordinary—goal for the *Ask Formula*, which extends far beyond me or my company. It's a goal that's so big and so "out of the box" that I'm almost embarrassed to tell you, because it may seem impossible... *now*.

But hear me out.

You see, it's my vision that the *Ask Formula* will change the way e-commerce is conducted online—globally, and possibly forever. In fact, my vision is quite simple.

My vision is that every homepage in the world will someday have a *Survey Funnel*.

And my mission is to make sure "someday" is someday *soon*. The pay-off of this being that customers are always satisfied because sellers are always providing what they really want. Sellers are then *always* profiting from meeting the needs of their customers.

That is my vision. *That* is my reason for publishing this book.

Do I believe it's possible? *Absolutely.*

Do I believe this is going to take some time? *You bet.*

This book is the first step.

And the most exciting thing is this: *You* get to be part of this movement.

And even more exciting?

Is the fact that this is something you can *feel good* about being part of. Because the *Ask Formula* is one of those rare opportunities to simultaneously benefit merchants and consumers—and in a profound way that can change the digital landscape forever.

You see, I'm giving it all away in this book, *Ask*. I'm seeding the field to help make it possible. And not only that, but it's my hope that you will apply the *Ask Formula*, refine it, and improve it so it can grow and take on a life of its own. In fact, as my mentor Dr. Glenn Livingston said in his Foreword, he invested his time, energy, and resources in coming up with a formula and then I was able to grab the baton and take it to the next level. It's my hope (and I know his as well) that you will now do the same thing.

In fact, let's talk about how to do that. Let's talk about where to go from here.

CHAPTER TWENTY-TWO

Next Steps

Now It's Your *Turn to Ask*

So, where do you go from here? What do you do next?

Well, for starters, it's all about *starting*. It's not about getting it perfect; it's about getting it *going*. Take what you've taken away from this book, and start putting it into action—today.

And as far as what to *specifically* do next, I would be remiss not to end this book with a *Pivot Survey* of sorts help give you some guidance. To help you decide which *specific Next Step* is right for you. As far as what to do next, here are your options:

OPTION #1: GET ACCESS TO THE SOFTWARE

If you feel like you've got a good grasp of the *Ask Formula* methodology and you're ready to jump in and create your first *Survey Funnel* yourself, then you might want to start by checking out and getting access to our *Survey Funnel Software* by visiting *http://www.SurveyFunnelSoftware.com*.

OPTION #2: GO DEEPER INTO THE METHODOLOGY

If you love the concepts in this book, but you're the type of person who likes to see how to complete each step of the process through step-by-step video instruction (or to arm your team with step-by-step instructions to implement), then you might want to check out our comprehensive, digital *Survey Funnel Course*, which goes into much more detail than we could ever possibly cover in a written book, by visiting: *http://www.SurveyFunnelCourse.com*.

OPTION #3: SEE OTHER BUSINESSES USING THE ASK FORMULA
If you'd love to see examples of the *Ask Formula* in action, and to connect with other like-minded business owners who are implementing the *Ask Formula*, as well as get access to *additional* training from world class business and marketing experts designed to take your business to the *next level,* then you might want to check out our online *Next Level Group Mastermind,* by visiting: *http:// www.NextLevelGroupMastermind.com.*

OPTION #4: WORK DIRECTLY WITH ME AND MY TEAM
Or finally, if you'd like to work directly with me and my team, or have our Funnel Specialists Agency do all the work for you— conduct your *Deep Dive Survey,* design your entire *Survey Funnel,* create all the pages and emails, write all the copy, and even manage your traffic, this is what we do all day, every day. You can find out how to work with us by visiting *http://www.FunnelSpecialists.com.*

■ ■ ■

Whichever option is right for you, the most important thing is to *start.* Take action *now,* while this is on your mind and you're thinking about it. You're armed with everything you need to take the next step. The only question is this: *Are you ready?*

Because now it's your turn to *Ask.*

GLOSSARY

1-Click Upsell The process of selling an additional product to a customer with one click of a button

80/20 Principle Principle that states 80% of your results will come from 20% of your effort, 80% of your revenue will come from 20% of your customers, etc.

Affiliate Referring to other businesses or people involved with selling your product for a commission on each sale

Ask Formula™ Formula used to survey prospects for determining their wants, needs and desires to sell your product or service

Autoresponder (AR) Series of emails sent automatically to a prospect or customer once they have opted in to receive emails from you

Avatar Composite description of your ideal prospect based on factors such as age, gender, income and occupation

Buckets The segmentation of your prospects based upon the problems they reveal when they answer your survey questions

Call to Action (CTA) When you ask or direct your prospect to make a decision or commitment. This could be making a purchase, entering in their email or clicking a link. Normally the CTA comes at the end of your copy

Case Study Example of how a person or business achieved a certain result through using the Ask Formula

Checkout Page Page on your website where the customer purchases your product or service

Coding system System of programming that allows you to organize information about your prospect as it relates to designing and building your Survey Funnel™

Cold traffic Visitors to your website that have no prior knowledge of you or your business who are visiting your site for the first time

Consumption Sequence The email sequence where your customer begins to use the service or product they purchased from you. Typically this involves sending them messages about how they can maximize the value of their purchase through email messages or other forms of correspondence

Convert / Conversion	The act of taking a non-paying prospect to a paying customer within your sales funnel
Customer	Someone who has purchased from you (as opposed to Prospect, who is someone in your sales funnel who has not purchased from you)
Database	List of individual customers and prospects you have the ability to communicate with, for the purposes of the Ask Formula™ typically via email
Deep Dive Survey™	Describes the open-ended survey questions that allow you to deeply understand your market's needs. These questions require descriptive, often open-ended answers about your market's challenges and situation as opposed to a "yes or no" answer
Do You Hate Me Survey™	Survey questions that determine why your prospect did not buy your product or service
Downsell	Term that describes offering your prospect a "nearly as good" product with less features and benefits for a lower price
Email Follow-up Feedback Loop	Series of emails that follow up with both buyers and non-buyers in order to solicit feedback, which is used both for future communication and to revise your sales messaging
Ethical Bribe	Using a free or low cost item to entice your prospect to opt-in to your survey funnel
Exit Lander	Window that "pops up" directing viewers of your sales video to a text-based salesletter if they stop watching your sales video
Feedback Loop Series	Email sequence sent to buyers who did not purchase your upsell product or service
Funnel	See Sales Funnel
Grease the Wheels Question	Refers to a low threshold question that requires little thought on the part of your prospect. Example of this could be, "Are you a male or female?" These questions help us acquire the basic information we need for understanding our prospect
Headline	Opening statement of a landing page or email designed to acquire your prospect's attention and interest

Hook	The big marketing idea that pulls people into your Sales Funnel; it should simultaneously generate curiosity and desire in your prospect's brain
Hyper-responsive	Term that refers to the top 20% of survey takers of your Deep Dive Survey™ according to SCORE, which represents the segment of your market most likely to purchase a paid solution solving the problem you've surveyed about
Landing Page	The first page on your website where your prospect lands after clicking an online advertisement, search engine listing, email link or similar traffic source
LEN (Length)	Excel formula that stands for length to determine the potential value of a prospect based on the length of their survey responses
List	Refers to your list of email subscribers (see Database)
Marketing Funnel	See Sales Funnel
Mastermind	Group of expert entrepreneurs who collaborate to help one another solve common problems
Micro-Commitment	Small, non-threatening actions taken by your prospects that help you determine how best to fulfil their needs
Micro-Commitment	Bucket Survey™ Survey designed to use micro-commitments to determine which bucket, or prospect group a website visitor best fits into
MULT (Multiplier)	Excel function that stands for multiplier where you can determine the quality SCORE of each prospect in your survey funnel
Next Level ELITE	Exclusive group of Next Level Mastermind members who meet in person to massively grow their business
Next Level Group Mastermind	Online mastermind group run by Ryan Levesque for business owners looking to implement the Ask Formula; The group brings in weekly business experts, includes regular implementation workshops, and is an arena to both share and see how other business owners are successfully applying the techniques taught in this book.
Offer	The product or service you will provide to a prospect in exchange for their email address of purchase

One Time Offer (OTO)	Limited offer you present to a prospect that will only be offered once at any given time
Pareto Principle	See 80/20 Principle
Pay Per Click (PPC)	Method of advertising where you pay a certain amount of money for each time a prospect clicks to your website or landing page
Personalization Question	Survey questions that help you gain personal information about your prospect including factors like age and gender
Pivot Survey™	Survey designed to redirect your prospects and customers into a new direction by asking them what they're interested in learning about next
Post-Survey Sales Prescription	Method use to immediately sell to your prospect once they have filled out your Micro-Commitment Bucket Survey™
Problem, Agitate, Solution	Sequence of explaing how a problem relates to the prospect's situation, hitting their emotions surrounding the problem and introducing a solution
Profit Maximization Sequence	Process of selling complimentary items to your customer once they have purchased a product to maximize the value of each individual customer
Prospect	Individual who has entered your sales funnel and has not yet purchased something from you (compare to Customer)
Prospect Self-Discovery Landing Page Survey™	Landing page with a Micro-Commitment Bucket designed for your prospect to discover something about themselves
Sales Acceleration Series	Email sequence used to increase your prospect's urgency to purchase, sent if the first few emails in your autoresponder sequence did not convert the prospect into a paying customer
Sales Funnel	The series of steps you want people take to go from being a potential customer to becoming an actual customer in your online business
Sales Letter	Letter typically found on a website designed to persuade a prospect into buying. Sales letters are formatted to read much like a letter from another person
Sales Page	A webpage which hosts your Sales Letter or Video Sales Letter

Same Visit Sale (SVS) Process of selling to your prospect immediately after they have taken your Micro-Commitment Bucket Survey™

SCORE Scoring formula used in the Deep Dive Survey™ process to identify and rank your most hyper-responsive survey-takers in descending order, starting with most hyper-responsive

Segment (n.) Refers to market segment (e.g. women vs. men)

Segment (v.) Refers to the act of separating prospects into different "buckets" based on certain types of criteria, so you can market to those buckets in a more specific, tailored way

Segmentation Question Survey question used to determine which bucket your prospect should be placed in

SMIQ (Single Most Important Question) Question in the Deep Dive Survey™ that determines what the top challenge is facing your prospect

Soft Sell Story Series Email series that makes use of storytelling as a means to sell your product or service

Sub-buckets Segmenting your prospects within their original buckets based on more specific challenges they face

Sub-Segment Refers to a sub-group within a market segment (e.g. women who have children, where women is the segment, and women with children is the sub-segment)

Survey Funnel Software Software used to automate your SurveyFunnel™

Survey Funnel Strategy Marketing strategy that uses four different surveys to improve your sales conversion rates

Thank You Page Webpage where prospects and customers are thanked for completing a specific call to action, like opting into your email list or purchasing your product

Themes Refers to the broad categories of survey responses discovered through the Deep Dive Survey™ process

Upsell Process of selling a complimentary product or service after your customer has bought your initial product or service

Upsell / Cross-Sell Sequence Email sequence to sell an additional product or service to your customers who have purchased your initial product

Video Sales Letter (VSL)	Sales letter presented in video format as opposed to text format typically using a PowerPoint display
Webinar	A training seminar or sales presentation delivered online, in which the presenter shares their screen - often displaying a PowerPoint presentation
Welcome Email	Email sent to a prospect or customer after they have completed a specific call to action such as completing your Micro-Commitment Bucket Survey™

ACKNOWLEDGMENTS

They say it takes a village to raise a child, and in many ways writing a book like this takes a village. In the case of *this* book, the village was more like an entire metropolis, and I am both humbled and overwhelmed by the number of people who have generously supported me personally in this journey, and who have supported this book. It would be impossible to thank everyone who had an impact, but there are a few people who deserve specific mention, because without them, this book simply would not have been possible.

My family is at the top of that list, starting with my incredibly supportive wife, Tylene, who spent *many* nights and weekends caring for our two young boys Henry and Bradley while I was burning the midnight oil to finish this manuscript—and building the company to execute the *Ask* vision. She doesn't get the same level of public recognition, but I can unequivocally say without her by my side, none of what you've read would have even been remotely possible.

My parents, Paul and Joanne Levesque, and my sister Allison Levesque have always been there since the beginning with unconditional love, even today as we're spread across the country. My wife's family, especially my sister-in-law, Clara Bautista, and mother-in-law, Maria Bautista, so many times have dropped everything to help out and come to the rescue, like when I was hospitalized in the ICU. Thank you, I love you all.

Next on the list is Karen Anderson. Thank you Karen, for believing in me, being this book's number one champion since day one, and for having a vision bigger than I could see. The thousands of hours you put into this book is something that will never be forgotten—a debt I'll never be able to repay. From the bottom of my heart, thank you.

So many more people helped with this book starting with my good friend Ronnie Nijmeh who helped inspire me to write this book in the first place, as well as my publisher David Dunham who took a chance on a first-time author, and to the whole Dunham Books team—specifically Joel Dunham and Crystal Flores.

Thank you also to Erica Gordon-Mallin, and Shawn Dady, as well Ron Reich and Colin Theriot for all your help with this manuscript. Will Hamilton and Ross Bridgeford, thank you for openly sharing your success and inspiring others to follow in your footsteps. And thank you to Steve Anderson for providing many hours of support and to Sissi Haner (editor extraordinaire), as well as Ani Poddar and your team in India for providing lightening fast support services.

So many teachers, mentors, coaches, partners, and colleagues believed in this book and supported its message, many of whom I'm humbled to call friends, starting with Brian Kurtz, who has opened so many doors and introduced me to so many people. It would be impossible to thank you enough here.

A special thank you to my single most important mentor— Dr. Glenn Livingston; my long-time friend and software partner Jack Born; and our Oceans Four brothers, Andre Chaperon and Ben Settle. Dan Meredith, you define loyalty and commitment. Jeff Walker, Perry Marshall, and Joe Polish: I never imagined the opportunity not only learn from you, but also work with you. Todd Brown: to me, our bond is brotherly. James Schramko, my coach, sounding board, and truth teller. Keith Baxter, Curt Maly, Dr. Harlan Kilstein, Howie Jacobson, Andy Hussong, for seeing the potential in something *before* it took off.

David Deutsch, David Garfinkel, Kevin Nations, Danny Iny, Derek Johanson, John McIntyre, Marisa Murgatroyd, Murray Gray, Gauher Chaudhry, Greig Wells, and Jonathan Mizel—thank you all.

Jay Abraham, John Carlton, Dan Kennedy, Tim Ferriss: you changed my path in life in ways I could never describe. And thanks to Jon Shugart, Darren Casey, Marci Lock, Doberman Dan Galapoo, Keith Krance, Mike Buontempo, Mike Colella, Selena Soo, Esther Kiss, Tiji Thomas, Robert Coorey, Ryan Lee, Ana Hoffman, Charles Kirkland, Kevin Rogers, Daniel Marama, and Steve Rosenbaum.

Dave Gonzalez, thanks for putting me on stage before I was a somebody.

Thanks to Michael Lovitch, Rob Jones, and Jon Benson. And Bond and Kevin Halbert, for keeping your father's legacy alive and brilliance available to the world. Thank you Brad Costanzo, Ryan DiParisi, Princess Fizz, Daryl Urbanski, Phoebe Chongchua, John Lee Dumas, Ross Andrews, Josh Turner, Jason Drohn, Justin Christianson, Matt Gill, Rachel Kersten, Mark Thompson, Carl Picot, Jake Hower, Jack Mize, Brian Horn, and David Frey.

Mike Hill, thanks for spreading and supporting the vision without agenda or expectation. And thanks to Jimmy Harding, James Reynolds, Dr. Jeremy Weisz, Tim Paige, Adil Amarsi, Matt Williams, Antonio Perez, Sweeney Daniels, Clint Evans, Steve Siegwalt, Jack Humphrey, Gina Gaudio-Graves, Jaime Tardy, Camari Ellis, Kevin Jordan, Joel Louis, Eric Loftholm, Nicola Cairncross, Christy Haussler, Anthony Tran, Farnoosh Torabi, Mark Summers, Tim Goodwin, Mike Rhodes, Jared Ermin, and Jason Henderson.

Neville Medhora for inspiring me to leave the corporate rat race. John Logar, Tim Francis, and Annie Pratt who offered such invaluable leadership, guidance and support, each in your own special way.

There are many others not on this list who should be. You know who you are. I wish I could have held out this manuscript indefinitely to add each and every new name of those who stepped up to support this project each and every week. Know that I know what you've done, and I am so grateful for your support.

Thank you to all the members of my family who supported me along the way including Matante Judy, Michelle Rancourt, Matante Charlotte, Uncle Bob, and Erica Fortin. Thanks to my best friend, Curtis Greenwood, with whom I learned the joy of making up the rules and taking the road less traveled. My college roommate, Dr. Charles Kassardjian, my Beta Rho brothers, and the early mentors in my life who did more to help me get here than they may have ever realized, including Dr. Paul Winchester, Misha Joukowsky, Josef Mittlemann, and Peter Flint.

Special thanks to my entire incredible team, especially Kimberly, Ian, Yassin, Andy, Dan, Dave, Darren, Robert, Ron, and Kory.

Without you guys this would be nothing but a vision. You are the *true* leaders.

And last, but certainly not least, thank you to all my private clients, our agency clients, Next Level ELITE™ coaching students, Next Level Group Mastermind™ members, and every single customer who is putting the *Ask Formula* into action. You are changing the online landscape as we know it, and you continue to stretch me, inspire me and teach me every single day. This one is for you. Thank you.

ABOUT THE AUTHOR

In 2008, armed with nothing but a $450 laptop, an Ivy League background in neuroscience, and an insatiable curiosity to understand why people buy, Ryan Levesque left a lucrative career on Wall Street and later in Shanghai, China, to launch his first online business. After struggling initially and losing everything, he eventually went on to build a multi-million dollar online publishing business selling information and software using what's now become the *Ask Formula*.

Since then, Ryan has used the *Ask Formula* to help build *multi-million dollar businesses in 23 different industries* ranging from sports instruction to business funding to satellite television, generating over $100 million dollars in sales in the process. Today, he and his team offer training, consulting, and implementation services for entrepreneurs and businesses at all levels. Ryan resides in the Austin, Texas area with his wife, Tylene, and their two sons.